More Praise for WANDER WOMAN

"I knew this book would speak to th e-preneurs we coach, but I was deligh nt for my own transformation at midl ol-league, for this beautiful expression and pathway to freedom."

—Darelyn "DJ" Mitsch, President, The Pyramid Resource Group, and author of *The Team Advantage*

"High-achieving women are a special breed, and Marcia holds the key to giving you the meaning and satisfaction you are looking for. This book is like a treasure map—leading to the genius within you that is yet untapped."

—Laura Berman Fortgang, author of *Now What?* and *The Little Book on Meaning*

"Exhilarating! *Wander Woman* makes clear the core of restlessness many women experience—the will to ask, 'Is this all there is?'—and then leads them to discover the greatest gifts they have to offer and a source of transformative change."

—Sally Helgesen, author of *The Female Advantage* and coauthor of *The Female Vision*

"This is one of the best books I've ever read about women: it really helps to legitimize our journey and turn our restlessness into a strategy. It is also an important read for those who work with women now and in the future."

—Beate Heller, PhD, Group Head—Executive Development, Swisscom, Berne

"In life's pressures to perform—to be perfect—we lose our sense of self. This book helps all women who strive to achieve to get closer to their personal truths. Always hungry, always yearning, this internal journey is the next adventure."

—Betty Scharfman, Vice President, Marketing and Channel Management, WorldatWork

"Marcia Reynolds has been a force in the coaching world for over a decade. In *Wander Woman*, she offers her wit and wisdom to smart, driven women. The book is full of powerful coaching questions and exercises that help women to define their paths, channel their energy, and enjoy the ride along the way."

—Sandy Vilas, CEO, Coach U, Inc.

"For us who have attained 'success' but still yearn for a greater sense of contribution and purpose, this is *the* book. Using her well-honed coaching skills, Marcia cuts through the standard self-help jargon and lays out a process for moving from success to significance."

—Eileen McDargh, President, McDargh Communications, and author of *Gifts from the Mountain*

"Based on extensive, original research, *Wander Woman* provides sage advice on how to rise to the highest levels of success while maintaining one's core spiritual and emotional center. This is a must-have guide for a new generation of high-performing women."

—Jeffrey E. Auerbach, PhD, President, College of Executive Coaching

"Marcia Reynolds speaks to the heart and soul of every woman who is looking for purpose in her life. Through the pages of this book you will come to know her as a friend and mentor, there to guide you to the path that is right for only you."

—Suzanne Bates, author of *Motivate Like a CEO*

"Marcia Reynolds offers tremendous insights and a great approach for high-achieving women to define success in their own terms, chart their course, and achieve their fullest potential. From her own personal experiences and the real-life lessons of others, Marcia delivers that 'something more' that so many women have been looking for."

—Debra Boelkes, founder and CEO, Business Women Rising

"Marcia has her finger on the pulse of the modern-day high-achieving career woman, clearly identifying the restlessness and eternal search for recognition that so many women repeat endlessly throughout their careers. Her insights into how to engage and retain high-achieving women should be read by CEOs around the world."

—Kate O'Reilly, Director, Optimiss, Sydney, Australia

"Reynolds provides a compelling narrative about the underlying restlessness that afflicts many high-performing women. Grounded in her remarkable personal story, substantive research, and perspective gleaned from decades of corporate experience, the book will be meaningful to women (and men!) engaged in personal transformation."

—Doug Silsbee, author of *The Mindful Coach* and *Presence-Based Coaching*

WANDER WOMAN

Wander Woman

How High-Achieving Women Find Contentment and Direction

MARCIA REYNOLDS

BK®

Berrett–Koehler Publishers, Inc.
San Francisco
a BK Life book

Berrett-Koehler Publishers, Inc.
235 Montgomery Street, Suite 650
San Francisco, CA 94104-2916
Tel: (415) 288-0260 Fax: (415) 362-2512 www.bkconnection.com

Ordering Information
Quantity sales. Special discounts are available on quantity purchases by corporations, associations, and others. For details, contact the "Special Sales Department" at the Berrett-Koehler address above.
Individual sales. Berrett-Koehler publications are available through most bookstores. They can also be ordered directly from Berrett-Koehler: Tel: (800) 929-2929; Fax: (802) 864-7626; www.bkconnection.com
Orders for college textbook/course adoption use. Please contact Berrett-Koehler: Tel: (800) 929-2929; Fax: (802) 864-7626.
Orders by U.S. trade bookstores and wholesalers. Please contact Ingram Publisher Services, Tel: (800) 509-4887; Fax: (800) 838-1149; E-mail: customer.service@ingrampublisherservices.com; or visit www.ingrampublisherservices.com/Ordering for details about electronic ordering.

Printed in the United States of America

Berrett-Koehler books are printed on long-lasting acid-free paper. When it is available, we choose paper that has been manufactured by environmentally responsible processes. These may include using trees grown in sustainable forests, incorporating recycled paper, minimizing chlorine in bleaching, or recycling the energy produced at the paper mill.

Library of Congress Cataloging-in-Publication Data
Reynolds, Marcia.
Wander woman : how high-achieving women find contentment and direction / by Marcia Reynolds.
p. cm.
Includes bibliographical references and index.
ISBN 978-1-60509-351-2
1. Women executives—Psychology. 2. Job satisfaction. 3. Quality of work life. 4. Career plateaus. 5. Career development. I. Title.
HD6054.3.R487 2010
658.4′09082—dc22 2010008225

First Edition
15 14 13 12 11 10 10 9 8 7 6 5 4 3 2 1

I dedicate this book to my mother,
who never had a chance to live out her dreams.
I wish she were here to see me living out mine.

CONTENTS

PREFACE

This book is for you, Wander Woman. You represent the new face of high-achieving women who started moving into management positions about twenty-five years ago. You are different from the women who came before you. You are more confident, assertive, and active. Instead of hiding behind your desk, you put yourself on the front lines by constantly convincing, persuading, calculating, demonstrating, creating, and braving your way through corporate hallways. Your manager may label you rebellious and competitive. You see yourself as passionate. In your mind, you weren't hired to be efficient; you were hired to change the world. If your style becomes more of a problem than an asset, the difficulty doesn't last for long. As soon as you feel you can no longer make a significant impact in your domain, you move to another department or company. Or, you decide you can more easily change the world by being your own boss.

On the surface, this lifestyle sounds exciting. You start each new job with grand visions for what you can accomplish. Then reality hits and the job disappoints. Too often, you are pigeonholed, underutilized, micromanaged, and told to slow down. You spend more time planning exit strategies than you do envisioning your career. Somewhere along the way, the excitement turns into cynicism. The more you wander, the more likely you are to lose your sense of purpose and possibly your sense of self.

"I'm running out of options," Kali, age thirty-nine, told me. "I start a job with great anticipation, move up quickly, and then somewhere along the line, I wake up with this gnawing sense that it's over. The work isn't meaningful anymore. My boss avoids me because he can't give me what I want. So I start making plans to leave." I asked Kali if she had ever tried to change the organization instead of rearranging her life. She answered, "That's a battle I don't want to fight."

I have observed this shift in the demeanor of high-achieving women firsthand through my years of coaching female top talent and in the women attending my leadership classes worldwide. Year after year, the women I work with are more hopeful and bold than ever before. They are also more stressed and perplexed about their futures. When I tried to find resources I could share with my clients to help them better understand themselves and their choices, I found none. Management training and, sadly, many women's development programs have yet to fully recognize the shift. Classes and business books for women still focus on helping them find their voice, balance their life, or strategize their way to the top of their organization. My clients don't need to find their voice; they know how to roar. They don't expect to balance their life; they long to find peace in the chaos. They aren't focused on organizational politics; they want significant projects they can run with or businesses they can run on their own. More than anything, they seek to know what they can accomplish in this lifetime without feeling exhausted and lonely in the end.

The shift is so profound you might call it a revolution, but no one has ventured to name what is happening. You might not have realized that thousands of women have the same burning issues and desires that you have and seek contentment and direction as you do. My clients are also surprised to hear how many other women face the same challenges as theirs. They are glad to know you exist, too. Together, you can bring the revolution to light.

To help increase this awareness and fill in the gaps of

understanding, I chose to do my doctoral research on what today's high-achieving women are doing in the workplace that keeps them from achieving executive positions. My research included multiple surveys with one hundred women between the ages of twenty-nine and fifty-two in the United States who fit my profile for "high achiever," plus ten intensive interviews with a random sample. The details of the study are described in the back of this book. More than half of the women were married and most of these women had children, so there was a balance between single women and those with families.

What I discovered through my surveys and interviews was that today's high-achieving women care less about the boardroom than they do about their strong desire to contribute. They have a longing for motion and meaning that often doesn't synchronize with the vertical ascent up the corporate ladder that so many people expected of them—and that they had expected of themselves when they started their careers. Therefore they often intentionally take themselves out of the running for leadership positions as they wander around looking for the elusive "something more" they need to do in this lifetime.

The paradox is that although the women feel confident about their choices, they are plagued by their restlessness. This "soulful agitation" leads them to accomplish great things but it leaves them aching for what's missing. They constantly question the value of their jobs, the definition of their purpose, the certainty of their identity, and their roles as wives, mothers, and sisters. Yet they still feel justified in keeping their lives in motion. It wasn't until I began writing this book that I found myself calling this group of women "Wander Women." The urge to move, mentally if not physically, is lodged in their souls. If they don't geographically move, they seek to change the landscape with new projects at work or at home, including a wide variety of volunteer commitments. Yet in spite of their constant drive for fulfillment, they long for contentment and peace of mind. The first question I wanted to answer after I completed my research was, “What tools for both success and happiness can I provide these women beyond writing a new resume?”

I wrote this book to offer the guidance and support you and your fellow strong, smart, and passionate sisters have been missing using methods I’ve been able to test with high-achieving women worldwide. In addition to my extensive research, I have decades of experience coaching women one-on-one and as a part of leadership development classes I teach for multinational companies. I also speak at conferences for women and I interact with women through blogging and teleseminars. My research and experience helped me to refine the techniques I offer and to provide case studies to assist you in adapting the techniques in this book.

The exercises and strategies in this book are enhanced by my own experiences as a leader, an employee, a high-achieving woman, a family member, and, finally, as a wayward teenager who rebelled against the standards and expectations others were setting for me. The lessons I learned during this very dark period gave me special insights on what it takes to re-create a life. I share my own stories in this book because all the research I have done and the intellectual wisdom I have gathered mean very little without facing my self-deception. Because I am asking you to make the same hard examination for yourself, I feel it is important to share my own journey. Be prepared to go on a more intense journey of transformation than you would when reading a typical “how to” book touting easy steps for success. I guarantee the results to be more lasting and fulfilling.

After the “dark days” of my twenties, I accumulated degrees, experience, and certifications that helped me formulate the content of this book, with coaching being most significant. My corporate positions were in training and organizational development departments. I experienced the typical frustration of watching people participate with gusto in a training class but then, when back on the job, apply very little of what they had learned. In my search for new techniques, I enrolled in a coaching school in 1995. I quickly saw the power of coaching to make the mental shifts required before behavioral change can occur. My passion for coaching led me to help establish the International Coach Federation (ICF), hold the position of president of the ICF in 2000, and become one of the first hundred people in the world to hold the certification of Master Certified Coach. I have woven in powerful coaching questions and techniques throughout this book to both motivate and maintain the commitment to change.

In the late 1990s, Daniel Goleman's book *Emotional Intelligence* led me to dig deeper into the brain research being done that was redefining how we mentally process new information.[1] I felt I had discovered one more important step in helping people make behavioral changes. To satisfy my hunger for knowing more, I chose to get my doctorate in organizational psychology. Every paper I wrote gave me deeper insights into my life choices as well as into the struggles many of my female coaching clients were experiencing. My doctoral work helped me to define "the burden of greatness" that high achievers now experience and the steps for Appreciative Dialogue (see chapter 5) to help them carry forward what is good in their lives to resolve their urgent issues. These are crucial concepts to the flow of this book. My dissertation research helped me to further define the needs of high-achieving women. Throughout the book, I share the most illuminating stories, quotes, and themes that were revealed in my research.

Finally, I decided to go beyond just sharing my research with my clients and write this book after rereading the epilogue to Margaret Wheatley's book *Leadership and the New Science*. Wheatley describes the need for community when she says, "We can turn to one another as our best hope for inventing and discovering the worlds we are seeking."

Most of my coaching clients are lone rangers who rarely reach out to other women in their organizations unless they are required to in a formal program. Wheatley advocated connecting, not just networking, to test out and share new ideas, listen to one another's stories, and encourage one another when disappointments loom. "We need each other differently now. We cannot hide behind our boundaries or hold onto the belief that we can survive alone."[2] Wheatley's words inspired me to provide a forum for high-achieving women to learn and grow together. My hope is that many women will work through this book in groups, whether online or in live gatherings. My wish is to rally the strength and wisdom of my high-achieving sisters so that none of us ever loses our way again.

WHAT YOU WILL FIND IN THIS BOOK

This book is intended to help you answer the questions you ask while you wander. I am not trying to convince you to act differently. Instead, I hope to shift your awareness and awaken you to a world of possibilities beyond your daily perspective. This means you can't just read through the book, talk about the concepts, and determine if you agree or not. You have to spend time reflecting on the pages, completing the exercises, dialoguing with a friend or coach about what you've learned, and having the courage to try out behaviors in opposition to your habits. Then you can determine if you agree with what I present or not. If you are ready, your questions will be answered. "Will I ever find peace of mind in the moment? Will I ever feel that the work I've done is good enough? How can I know if I am doing what I am meant to do as my purpose on this planet?" Once you have this awareness, it is irreversible. The objective of *Wander Woman* is not to teach you; the goal is to transform you.

In part I of the book, chapter 1 starts by exploring what differentiates you from the women who came before you to clarify your own needs and desires. The second half of chapter 1 presents real-life quotes and stories to enhance the descriptions of both the light and dark sides of your typical behaviors. There are checklists you can use to determine how much of the Wander Woman archetype is actually in your blood. Chapter 2 defines the "burden of greatness." On the dark side of this restless pursuit of new challenges is the feeling that there is always something more to do. You meet a goal beyond expectations and then immediately say, "What's next?" I explore my personal experience with this phenomenon and how it played into the darkest period of my life. Then I share questions you can ask yourself to keep from carrying this burden in the future. You can live in harmony with your urge to wander and even use it to define your future if you better understand the source of your impulses.

Part II moves into the present with exercises and coaching questions to help you make an intentional transformation. Chapter 3 will help you discover your "circle of selves" that form who you are today and how you can expand who you can be tomorrow. Chapter 4 looks deeper inside your mind, where three assumptions form the mindset that keeps your perfectionist pattern locked in place. You have to acknowledge both the value and the harm of these three assumptions if you want any changes you attempt to last. You will also learn visioning techniques to help you reset your mental programming on a daily basis. Chapter 5 teaches you how to take advantage of the "window of opportunity" after any emotionally charged experience where you can step out of your frame and use Appreciative Dialogue and journaling to facilitate the renewal process. What you learn from these moments enriches your daily visioning routine. Finally, chapter 6 will help you discover what gives you a sense of purpose distinct from your need for recognition. When you passionately live with a strong sense of purpose, you can remember what is most important to you no matter how people judge you or what difficulties you face. When you practice the exercises, answer the questions, and implement the routines laid out for you in Part II, you will find the contentment and direction you seek.

Part III expands the process by helping you apply what you have learned to a broader life strategy. In essence, wandering can become your strategy instead of a series of unplanned upheavals. First, you need to actively sustain the transformation you began in Part II. Chapter 7 will give you four tools to help you overcome your tendency to find other things to do than the work of transformation. Chapter 8 then provides three scenarios where women used the techniques in this book to successfully climb the corporate ladder, navigate below the glass ceiling while still getting great assignments and recognition, and do a total life makeover. I share their stories in the hope that whatever strategy you choose, you move forward with clear intentions for what you want for your future. Chapter 9 gives you ideas and resources you can use if you choose to influence leaders in your workplace to support and engage top-talent women. Organizations will be more competitive if they understand how to cultivate and retain this amazing creative force.

I was working on my manuscript on a plane to Dallas, Texas, while sitting next to a thirty-something woman who was traveling with her four young children dispersed in the three rows around me. In a rare moment when she wasn't watching her children, she looked over my shoulder and asked me what I was writing. I reluctantly told her, assuming she was not my target audience. Shame on me for making this assumption. She launched into a diatribe about the struggles she is having with the business she owns with her current husband and how no adult seems to understand her even though she knows the risks she takes are right. Her children understand her best; they know that they need to stand back and drop in line when she decides to forge a new path. She said, "Oh, I'm a Wander Woman all right. And so is my sister. Do you really think this is a sort of tribe, or is it a sign of the future for women where we finally get to express who we are?" Bless this woman for giving me the questions I will address at the end of this book.

Based on this interaction, in chapter 10 you will reflect on the questions the woman on the plane asked me. After you experience the book, including the research, the questions, the exercises, and your reflections, I will ask you if you think Wander Woman represents a personality style or, instead, if you think she symbolizes something that is in all women, bubbling up to the surface as we progress. The answer is important not only to how you see yourself, but also to how you explain yourself, your desires, your vision, and your passion in the world. If you are a part of something bigger than yourself, you may be called to serve a higher mission of helping your wandering sisters succeed as well. Power is in the collective. We can make a substantial difference that benefits us all if we choose to rise up together.

This book is for you, Wander Woman. You can finally come home to rest your feet before the wind blows and takes you off on your next adventure. I hope you savor the ideas, the exercises, and the questions I offer. Take your time, keep your mind open, find other women to go through the process with you, and celebrate your successes. I wish you joy as well as clarity in the process.

Marcia Reynolds
Phoenix, December 2009

PART I

The Quiet Revolution

ONE

The Road to Somewhere

A few years ago, I was listening to a luncheon speaker talk about the difference between what is most important to men and women in the workplace. He said men tend to focus on career and how they can drive their way up the ladder. Then, for numerous reasons, they shift to focusing on intimacy as they age. On the other hand, women focus first on intimacy. As they age and their children grow up, they focus on career. I said, "Not the women I know."

After three decades of training and coaching high-achieving women, I have noticed an evolution of their needs and desires. In the past, my female clients longed for life balance; now they get bored if their plate isn't full of new and exciting challenges where they can showcase their skills. Once they were desperate to overcome their fears; now they want help laying out a clear career path so they can quit making brash decisions. They used to ask for assertiveness skills; now they are looking for ways to better formulate their words so people will quit questioning them and get on board with their ideas. Women still face inequities in the workplace and difficulties juggling their many responsibilities. Yet something has changed in the women themselves, the way they approach life, the way they work, and the way they relentlessly show up even when they aren't sure what they are fighting for. In essence, the answer to the questions "who am I?" and "what does this all mean to me?" have changed. Instead of an evolution of behaviors from one generation of high-achieving women to the next, a revolution is going on as you read this page.

Few resources are available for this new force of women. Many self-help books advise women on what they should and shouldn't do to succeed. These books are based on old assumptions. Women today are very different from their pioneer predecessors and scoff at the idea that they resemble their mothers. With no guidelines for offering the support today's high-achieving women need to succeed, their managers are ill-equipped to develop and retain them. What's worse, the women don't know where to turn for help. Therefore, I'll share the old characterization of working women to see clearly what is causing frustration for women today. Then we'll explore the five pitfalls high-achieving women are faced with today and the possible negative behavior that could result. If you find you are saying, "Yes, that's me" as you read, know that you will be given specific steps for finding the satisfaction you desperately seek in the chapters that follow.

THE AGE OF THE IMPOSTOR

An important study was done in 1978 that found that, despite their gains, most accomplished women in the 1970s felt they weren't very smart and had fooled anyone who thought otherwise. They attributed promotions to "luck, timing, an overestimation of abilities and faulty judgment by decision makers."[1] Even if at some level these women knew they were intelligent, they were cautious about expressing their ideas. They calculated their moves and hedged their bets. It took years of experience before they claimed their own brilliance and creativity, if they ever did at all. The researchers referred to this behavioral pattern as the Impostor Phenomenon.

No matter how hard they worked, the women in the study felt they were impostors and never stopped worrying that they would be "found out" and ousted from their positions. They keenly protected their gains and cautiously called anyone "friend." On one end of the spectrum of behaviors, the women struggled with speaking up. They didn't ask for what they wanted; they hoped they would be recognized and given raises based on the quality of their work. If they didn't get what they hoped for, they quietly suffered, rarely making their desires known. On the other end of the spectrum, instead of acting passively, some women acted overaggressively. Behind their back, people called them names like Bully Broads and Ice Queens.[2] Meryl Streep brilliantly portrayed this archetype in the movie *The Devil Wears Prada*. Underneath their callousness, these women feared they would never be able to meet expectations and that other people were constantly trying to cheat them and steal their jobs. Instead of losing their voice, they acted as if they were superior to everyone else to cover their fears. Of course, what we see in the movies are women who play the stereotypes to an extreme, acting utterly submissive or brilliantly conniving. No matter where women fell on the spectrum in reality, the prevailing factor among most of the women in the workplace before the mid 1980s was a damaging lack of confidence. I find this trend still evident today when I teach in emerging countries and in Western industries still dominated by men. It's as if the Impostor Phenomenon is the first stage women go through when they start breaking down corporate doors.

WOMEN WHO HAD TO BE MEN

Although the Impostor Phenomenon was significant inside research circles, the issues discussed by nonacademic women in the workplace in the 1970s and 1980s centered on whether a woman should stay at home to raise children or choose to live and act more like a man. The middle ground was vague. Women who chose to work were told to "dress for success," so they donned traditional dark-skirted suits with shoulder pads. They were instructed to verbally fight like men and to talk about sports to gain acceptance. One company I worked for rated their "promotable" women based on an assessment that compared them to the top male leaders. The women then had to set goals to act more appropriately before they could be promoted.

As we moved into the 1990s, the self-help and seminar themes for businesswomen focused on work-life balance and rediscovering the feminine side they lost trying to be more like men. Even today, many women pay lots of money to go on retreats to de-stress or to "find their inner goddess."

The high levels of stress and the push to be acknowledged haven't changed. However, the answers and even the questions women are asking themselves in order to discover how to create happy, fulfilling lives are changing. Many high-achieving women no longer feel like Impostors. They no longer feel they have to dress, act, and talk like men. Yet who they are becoming is still unfolding. What today's high-achieving women need to feel happy is different from their predecessors. Until now, few guidelines were available to help them find their way.

> ***Julie, age thirty-four, said,*** *"I knew early on that I was going to make my own choices based on who I am and who I want to be. Yet these are hard criteria to identify."*

ENTER WANDER WOMAN

In 1991, senior executives at Deloitte & Touche found that only four out of fifty candidates for partner were women, even though they had been heavily recruiting women from colleges and business schools since 1980.[3] They didn't see the problem as a glass ceiling. If a woman applied to be partner, she stood a good chance of being chosen. Neither was the problem due to a lack of performance. Records showed the women performed as well as and in some cases better than the men. Women performed very well, until they left.

The problem was that significant numbers of women were leaving the firm before they could even be considered for partner.

The CEO at the time, Mike Cook, decided the high turnover of women was an urgent problem that needed to be fixed. His predominantly male executive team didn't agree. They assumed the women were leaving to stay home with their children and there was nothing they could do about it. Cook didn't settle for this answer. Against massive complaints about wasting time and money, Cook created a task force that started their research by interviewing women who had left the company.

The task force found that most of the women left because they felt management stifled their drive for achievement, not because they wanted to be home with their families. They felt devalued by not getting the best assignments, by not receiving mentoring, and by not feeling as if their managers knew who they really were. They said many male managers were overly protective, as if the women couldn't handle their lives on their own. The results revealed a more subtle discrimination than in previous decades. The women said the managers formed opinions about who they were and what they wanted without ever asking them. Within a few years, they tired of not being seen or heard and moved on to find greater and more fulfilling challenges.

Armed with this information, Cook created a plan for Deloitte that first focused on upgrading the perceptions of the current generation of women in their workforce. They didn't need to fix the women. They needed to fix their culture. In 2005, Deloitte selected 116 women as partners, principals, and directors, up from 3 in 1992.[4] The transformation is happening.

Deloitte was one of the first big corporations to discover that the current generation of high-achieving women is often misunderstood and generally mismanaged. Although the leaders claimed to provide a woman-friendly environment, they were actually stifling the spirit of the women they had aggressively recruited. The men thought they were helping the women. Instead, they were actually holding them back. Their views were not shifting fast enough to keep up with the changing needs and desires of the women. What most surprised the managers was that the top-performing women did not stay and fight. These days, strong women take their expertise and knowledge to greener pastures.

Today's high-achieving women are not giving up; if the workplace doesn't support their needs, they are choosing to move on.[5] Women typically have a high capacity to adapt if they want to, but the women who leave companies are choosing not to adapt. When companies quit showing gratitude for their high-quality work, these women begin looking elsewhere. If they stay during a down economy, they spend time planning their next move. As soon as the economy picks back up, they are gone. Their confidence in their abilities, their courage to take risks, and their disdain for "giving in" is greater than their fear of not finding another job.[6]

Whereas high-potential men tend to choose to stay with one company because of a sense of responsibility to their family, their female counterparts are more likely to ask their family to support their job-hopping decisions and find ways to work with the shifts in income, location, and schedules.[7] Half of the women in my study had children at home, yet they all spoke about various degrees of ease in leaving their jobs, from describing the process as "extricating myself" to simply saying, "next!" One of the women I interviewed went, in less than twenty years, from being a CPA in a big-four New York accounting firm, to an internal position handling international tax policy for a major telecommunications company, to being a lobbyist in Washington, to taking an executive position for a company so she could live on the California coast, all the while doing her favorite thing, teaching Pilates. She said, "I just feel that I have to move on."

Sue, age forty-eight, said, *"I never serve time. I have quit jobs because they were intrinsically not satisfying, they became too boring, or they asked me to focus on doing things I no longer found useful for my position and growth."*

In the United States, women today are also more inclined than men to switch industries as well as jobs, including starting their own businesses.[8] Women are also more likely to take the initiative to define new roles and jobs for themselves within a company. Sometimes they do a complete job "makeover" along the way, making the path look like a zigzag both horizontally and vertically. Their workplace wish lists rarely state "being promoted" as a prime motivator. Instead, my survey respondents told me they look for (1) frequent new challenges that stretch and grow their ability to achieve; (2) the opportunity to be flexible with their schedule; (3) the chance to collaborate with other high achievers; (4) recognition from their company; and (5) the freedom to be themselves.

Debbie, age forty-five, said, *"Moving up the corporate ladder doesn't appeal to me if I have to morph myself into being someone I'm not to get ahead. . . . I'm not sure what I want for my future but I am sure I want to proudly be me."*

The lack of frequent new challenges and learning opportunities has led many women around the world to use corporate experiences as a training ground to hone their skills in preparation for owning their own companies. Growth in the number of women-owned businesses has significantly outpaced that of overall businesses. By 2004, half of all privately held U.S. businesses in the top fifty metropolitan areas were women-owned.[9] The fastest-growing sectors include traditionally male-owned companies such as construction, transportation, and agricultural services. Women-owned businesses are also rising sharply around the world, even in countries that traditionally suppressed women, such as China, Russia, and Saudi Arabia. The emergence of confident, educated, and restless women is truly a global phenomenon.

THE ROAD NOW TAKEN HAS YET TO BE PAVED

Many of today's high-achieving women move around so much because their definition of success is not predetermined. Although they might like their titles and money, they feel these standard corporate rewards are a means to an end they haven't yet defined. They embody a drive toward mastery, yet they are constantly questioning what they want for their future. Sunny Hostin, a managing director in the New York office of the investigative firm Kroll Inc., a regular commentator on CNN, and the mother of two young children said, "Any woman who is successful will admit that you have to prepare for your next move; you always have to be thinking about it."[10] Ultimately, the range of choices offered by a company affects the decision to stay or opt out, a decision these women repeat over and over again because they won't suffer long in jobs that don't offer frequent new challenges and movement.

Therefore, when it comes to helping strong women make crucial choices for their careers and their lives, it is important to study their inner as well as their outer journey. Self-satisfaction seems to be more important to today's high achievers than the outer trappings of success. Yet how they create self-satisfaction isn't clear to them. This uncertainty leads them to continually question the road they are on. I'm reminded of what the Cheshire cat told Alice in Wonderland, "If you don't know where you are going, any road will do." What was the road less taken is now filled with passionate, driven women who question their direction and feel tired, anxious, and empty at the end of the day. It's time we put up some guideposts and refueling stations to help these women along the way.

I AM NOT MY MOTHER

I didn't know until after my mother died that the only inheritance she had received was a letter along with her mother's will saying, "Everything goes to your brother because you can find a man to marry and take care of you." Most of her life, my mother grudgingly sacrificed her needs for her brother. She couldn't go to college because there was only enough money for her brother's schooling. Her father died when she was five, so she spent most of her childhood working in the family clothing store when she wasn't in school. Her brother got to study and play sports. She moved with her mother and brother to Phoenix when she was twenty because of her brother's asthma. Two years later, her mother died. In the 1940s in Phoenix, Arizona, jobs were scarce for my mother's level of education and experience. They were even more limited for Jews. My mother eked out a living on her own until she married my father when she was twenty-three. She got pregnant a month later.

My mother never had a life of her own beyond raising her family. Although she did volunteer work, she never accomplished anything that received public acknowledgment as my father had. After we grew up and left, she spent most of her time caring for my sick father. I never felt close to her; she was either angry or emotionally distant. I didn't realize until I was much older that she wasn't angry with me. She died in her late sixties from complications due to dementia. Frankly, I think she just checked out.

Many of the women I interviewed felt their mothers were angry about not having a choice for how they wanted to live their lives. Some of the women had mothers with lifelong careers. Even then they felt their mothers took jobs more for the money they would make than for their own pleasure. Dinner conversations were not about the joy of work but about the pain of not being able to do their best at work. A person or rule always stood in their way. Their sense of helplessness kept them from being role models of power and actualization. If they were fighters, they sensed their battle was a lost cause. Sadly, a few of the women thought their mothers were jealous of their successes and criticized them more than they praised them.

> ***Julie, a thirty-four-year-old engineer, said,*** *"There was always competition between my mother and myself. My mother was held back in what she thought were her options. I think she needed to work. But it wasn't her chosen work and she always seemed drained. . . . I have lived my life 90 percent not wanting to be like my mother. There are great things about my mom, but her life in general and the way she approaches it is very different from the way I do."*

High-achieving women today are not willing to give up their personal satisfaction and sense of accomplishment as their mothers did. Although discrimination still exists in the workplace and women must still make trade-offs between their careers and family, there has been a drastic shift in norms around women's roles both at home and at work as well as a shift in women's own self-concept. It's true that juggling the responsibilities of family and home with their work life is still an issue. Many women choose flexible jobs that will allow them to "see their babies grow up." However, these women want to be good mothers *and* they want to be recognized for the value they give to the workplace. They can be a mother and a CEO if they choose to. They can be feminine and compete with the guys at the same time. Women can do what they want and get the recognition they deserve if they know what they want and deserve.

THE FUEL FOR WANDERING

Today's high-achieving women won't stand in anyone's shadow and would never aspire to be someone's assistant unless the job gave them autonomy, new challenges, and a chance to shine on their own in a reasonable amount of time. They don't apply for jobs; they seek opportunities. Once they earn a position, they aim to quickly accomplish their goals and just as quickly look around the corner for the next opportunity, which could be in the same company if there is space to grow. Their overall sense of confidence, pride in their work, and passion for life keep them moving forward.

> ***Elizabeth, age forty-one, said,*** *"I remember my father was talking about how he wanted his kids to take over his company. He says, 'And Elizabeth, you can be vice president.' What did he mean, vice president? Why wouldn't I be president? He says, 'Well the boys, they're men, and the industry is mostly men . . .' I remember being so mad at him for making that comment. It's not the way I was raised. He had always said, 'You can be anything you want to be!' So then he's said I couldn't be president? Well, he has since apologized 150 times for that day."*

Elizabeth explained that her father raised her to be a successful businesswoman. He had helped her create her first business card when she was twelve years old and taught her how to give a firm handshake and look people in the eye when she asked to be their babysitter. When she was sixteen, her father suggested she get a full-time job to earn experience. Instead of taking his suggestion, she chose a simple weekend job so she could take college classes. Since graduating from college, she has redefined her career three times, each time reaching the top of her job rank before deciding to move on. Currently, she makes more money than her father.

More than ever, women are making their own career choices and setting the terms for what they call success. If someone tries to keep them from getting what they want, they feel motivated to try even harder to prove they can succeed. Julie, age thirty-four, said, "My rebelliousness fuels me." She sees rebelliousness as her strength; her success is dependent on her strength of will.

Some people claim these women have a sense of entitlement. It's true they feel they are special. But they hit the ground running, working hard for what they earn. They feel they deserve to be valued, respected, recognized, and then given great projects to work on for their extra effort and superior performance even if they lack years of experience. They feel they deserve attention and perks as a result of their effort, which has nothing to do with their age. They strive to work harder than everyone else, they are willing to learn from their mistakes, and their accomplishments are excellent. They are outstanding performers—why shouldn't they feel entitled?

> ***Sue, age forty-eight, said,*** *"I always felt I knew as much if not more than my bosses and I should be recognized and rewarded for that. In return, they would get outstanding work from me, beyond expectations. I could help take the organization to the next level if they let me. When this was slow to come, I was irritated and restless. They weren't using my strengths and they weren't acknowledging my brilliance. How stupid could they be?"*

In fact, these women love to show that they can do something that someone else said they couldn't. Generally, they aren't trying to prove that they can do something difficult in spite of their gender; being a woman factors very little into their reasons for proving their worth. Mostly they are intent on achieving what others think is impossible or foolish for them to attempt regardless of the basis of the judgment against them.

> ***Julie, age thirty-four, said,*** *"Why did I choose to be an engineer? Honestly, to prove I am smart enough to be an engineer."*

> ***Beth, age thirty, said,*** *"I don't like someone else telling me what I can't do. Just when you think you know what's best for me . . . I'll do more."*

These women are not invisible like many of their mothers and older female bosses, yet they think they are invincible, which causes them problems personally and professionally. There is a "dark side of abundance" to their confidence, impulsiveness, and even their passion. They must honestly confront the barriers that are still in the workplace. And they must face their inner demons before they can find the peace they desperately seek. If they do this, their burdens can become joys and their restless spirit can become the passionate energy that helps them find, explore, and achieve their purposeful path.

THE FIVE DRIVERS OF WANDER WOMAN

As a second-generation high-achieving woman, five factors drive your success in the workplace. An old adage declares, "Our greatest strengths are our greatest weaknesses." Therefore, these five drivers are also the source of the pitfalls you should avoid. On the surface, these drivers define why you are so remarkable and shine above your colleagues. If you aren't careful, these drivers can also lead you to make decisions based on emotional needs instead of on a long-term plan or purpose, leaving you feeling aimless and discontent after a few frenzied decades.

In the following sections, I'll explain both the light and dark side of each driver to help you understand yourself, not to define yourself. You may not agree with all of the quotes and descriptions; see if your tendencies match up instead of rejecting the driver entirely if a specific behavior doesn't fit for you. I will also share anonymous quotes from women I surveyed so you can see the thought patterns that underlie the actions. Read the quotes out loud. *My intention is that you find in their words not only the strengths that have been instrumental to your success, but also the seeds of discontent that drain your happiness.* At the end of each section, I'll share how the negative behaviors related to each driver can sabotage your goals and dreams if you fall into these traps. You can use this information to create new beliefs and behavioral patterns using Part II of this book.

Driver 1. Extreme confidence

Give me a stick and I'll build you a bridge.

You feel you can do anything you put your mind to. The only time you are concerned about meeting a goal is after you accept a project and face the reality of your commitment, but even then doubt is fleeting. You are persistent, figuring out ways to bypass any "no" you are given. Ali, age thirty, said, "I'm either bold or defiant. I can't say for sure which drives me more." You get what you want but not out of gratuitous entitlement; you work hard for your wages, praises, and promotions. The adjectives you choose to describe yourself include: passionate, high-energy, persistent, assertive, direct, bold, and confident.

Some of your confidence comes from your focus early in life. Your parents did everything to make sure you would have a good future, which included excelling at school. Your self-worth centered on getting good grades and shining at extracurricular activities. If you had to work to help pay for your schooling, you found jobs easily. You had no doubt that you could support yourself. By the time you entered the workforce full-time, you felt highly confident about your abilities and you expected to move up fast in the organization.

Survey responses:

> *"My first two companies promoted me quickly to positions beyond my capabilities, both in experience and knowledge. But I rose to the challenge and figured it out."*

> *"I think the things that have happened to me in my life have been a matter of opportunity meets capability. I make things happen."*

> *"For a moment after I accept an assignment, I might gasp. In the end, I always figure it out and do it well."*

What is the dark side of being so confident?

- Taking on projects beyond your expertise and having to spend all your free time catching up.
- Never prioritizing because every project you do has to demonstrate how great you are. If you are taking on too many tasks, this can be overwhelming.
- Not seeing other possibilities while busily persisting down one path. Because of this, others may accuse you of not being strategic or visionary, which hurts your leadership potential.
- Steamrolling a project because you think you are right without broadly looking at the total impact on everyone involved.
- Risking an addiction to work—more and more, work becomes your priority over family, friends, and health, even when you say this isn't true.

Driver 2. Constant need for new challenges

Give me a stick and I'll build you a bridge,
unless I've already done that, so give me a
bigger challenge or I'll move on to something else.

You seem to have an internal flame that needs constant stoking. You seek successive accomplishments that are enjoyable to work on, whether you can do this in one company or you have to job-hop to get your needs met. If you feel you are not getting the recognition you deserve or that the work is becoming stale and boring, you begin your search for the next great thing. High salaries and stock options won't solely keep you in a position, though you might stay longer to make enough money to do what you really want to do, which is often to own your own business. Although you say you want peace of mind, your greater need is to accomplish things of value. You want to make a contribution, over and over again. You may experience fatigue from overworking and disillusionment with the corporate world, yet your passion and energy for creating amazing results doesn't wane with age. You want more peace and balance in your life . . . someday.

In a down economy, you might stay in a job a little longer than normal because fewer jobs are available. Yet you still keep your eyes and options open. You will even look in other industries for the right opportunity. You can always learn what you need to know on the job. What is before you has to be better than what you are leaving behind, even though you aren't clear about what you are getting into.

> *"I was never hired for a job I had done somewhere else. It was always a new challenge in a field I knew nothing about. It didn't scare me; it energized me."*

> *"I can walk into a situation and see where the holes are and what changes need to be made . . . then I do it. If I have the freedom to do that, I thrive."*

"I was always the top sales person. But then when I was done with sales, I knew I was done. When I started looking, I had no idea where I would end up. Yet I knew it would be great whatever it was."

The average length of time you spend in one particular job is about four years plus or minus two, even if you decide to stay with one company. Although you jump jobs by choice, your decision is usually based on *leaving something behind* instead of *choosing based on a plan*. By your mid-thirties, you regret not being more deliberate about your choices. You could have made a bigger difference if you had created a plan earlier in your life.

"Many times it would just be a matter of, 'been here, done that, I know how to do this, I have accomplished this, and it's time to sort of move on.' But then I never know what I'm going to do until the opportunity presents itself."

"I get so busy with activities that I don't get focused . . . do, do, do, always go somewhere, always do something, always travel, always have things in the works . . . but when I stop to take a breath, I feel shallow, like I'm not contributing to society. I'm not sure how to create what would make me feel more valued."

"I want to be free to make my own choices and decisions and not live by what someone else thinks is right for me. Is that enough of a purpose to have?"

What is the dark side of having a
constant need for new challenges?

- Feeling as though you've wasted time figuring out what you want to do.
- Making impulsive job choices based on what you don't want instead of what you want for the future, so some choices are good and some are not.

- Not stopping long enough to enjoy the fruits of success.
- Resenting jobs that started out well but failed to fulfill your needs over time.
- Not staying long enough in a company to earn an executive position where you could make significant changes to improve the organization.

Driver 3. A strong drive for recognition based on performance, not on gender

Don't do me any favors; just applaud me when I'm done.

You aren't trying to prove what a woman can do; being a woman factors very little into your reasons for proving your worth. You might experience sexual harassment and employment inequities in the workplace. You might even experience discrimination from older women who seem to be more interested in making you "pay your dues" than in supporting your rise in the company. Some of these acts are blatantly hostile and possibly illegal. However, instead of spending energy trying to eradicate the discrimination, you rev up your desire to succeed in spite of these roadblocks. You are driven to prove what *you* can do. If someone tries to keep you from succeeding, you feel provoked to prove your value even more.

> *"I proved them all wrong; I'm living the success they said I would never achieve."*

> *"They said I had to sleep with someone to get the job. I didn't, but I still had to endure dumb sexual comments and men looking up my skirt. When I moved to another unit, the discrimination wasn't so obvious but it was still there. Because I am good at what I do, they eventually backed off. It's a stupid game but as long as I know I can get my work done, I know I'll win in the end."*

"I have found that racial as well as gender discrimination is still alive and well. But it won't stop me from succeeding."

Because you are driven to perform, you have a direct communication style that can intimidate others and cause you to have political difficulties and interpersonal conflicts. Regardless of the personal nature of your motivation, you feel you are committed to obtaining outstanding results so your intentions should not be questioned. You are not self-serving. You serve the bottom line though your methods may be untraditional. Additionally, because you put more time and effort into finding the best way to do things than most people do, your voice should be heeded and respected. As a result, your communication style is very direct and passionate. This may serve you in a leadership role that requires a sense of urgency. However, regardless of the situation, this can cause rifts in your relationships. This doesn't mean you are self-absorbed and don't care about others. It means that people might not get to see your compassion. You often lose your patience if you feel someone is trying to pick a fight with you. You don't mind when people listen to your ideas and present good arguments in rebuttal if they have them, but you will compete if someone stands in your way.

"Even as a child I was very direct . . . I'm still the one who always says exactly what she's thinking. It does keep you out of some realms. I've been coached how not to do that, but it still happens."

"I was born spirited, full of will power. And when I'm stressed . . . I'm not the softest person around. . . . I was more abrasive and assertive than I might have needed to be. I thought I was being honest, but I guess I was being hurtful."

What is the dark side of having a strong drive to be recognized for your performance?

- Appearing insensitive to other people's needs, desires, and solutions.
- Reacting harshly to criticism.
- Others see your persuasiveness as intimidating.
- Holding people to high standards you create without tolerating differences.
- Coming across as argumentative, obstinate, and blunt when disagreeing with others.
- Not listening well unless you really want to.
- Allowing discrimination to continue if it's not stopping your progress.

Driver 4. Work is your life's blood

Retire? Never. I love knowing the world needs me.

Your greatest pleasure comes from your achievements in the workplace and out in the world. You couldn't imagine not working, which could include writing a novel or growing organic vegetables, unless you are thoroughly exhausted and physically need a break. It's not likely you will ever retire; your personal needs are met by completing projects well. Applying yourself to your work is how you get to be courageous, creative, self-sufficient, amazing, productive, outstanding, and the bold savior of all. You will never sit still, not even on a rainy holiday. You want to move mountains. That is the game you are playing and you want everyone to get out of your way.

Although you don't like to call yourself "competitive," you do measure yourself against people with greater successes than your own. You are driven to work even harder by the friend who got promoted faster, the colleague whose book hit the best-seller list, the neighbor whose Internet story went viral, and the competitor who found a new income stream. You may be happy for your friends but disappointed with yourself that they reached a pinnacle before you. If your peers have accomplished more than you have, you are driven to figure out how you can meet or beat their results. You don't do this for the pleasure of beating someone; you just want to know you have done your best.

> *"It's not so much that I need to sit a project on a shelf and say, 'I did this.' Once I've accomplished it I feel like, 'So, now what can I do?' I need to be invested and active to feel good about myself."*

> *"I could have saved the world yesterday, but if I haven't done anything today to make a difference, I feel like I am failing."*

> *"Whenever we have something new rolling out, I'm the first to get it done because I'm passionate. It's coming from my heart. It's not just about me."*

What is the dark side of making work your life's blood?

- Desiring peace of mind and balance but never creating the space for it.
- Being seen as arrogant instead of confident and self-serving instead of bighearted.
- Disconnecting with life outside of work.
- Caring so much about immediate results that you lose sight of the big picture.
- Able to deal with setbacks but not failures.

Driver 5. Experience is the best teacher

Kick me down, I'll bounce back up.
But that will never happen again.

You are often disillusioned by how work gets done, but you have the strength to rise up after every setback even if you must resurrect yourself elsewhere. One lesson you quickly learn is what kind of managers you like best to work for. If you receive little support for your progressive ideas, if you are told to "tone down" your energy, or if you feel held back in any way, you will either leave the company or create a new position for yourself as soon as you can. A *high-achiever-friendly* working environment is critical to retaining you. You learn your lessons quickly but you may not give your boss or the company a second chance.

This driver often leads you to believe you are self-sufficient and you don't need the advice or support of others. You learn fast. You adapt easily. You often appear wiser than everyone around you. This does not mean you don't need emotional support when the road gets bumpy. There are now many studies that prove that an active social network provides both mental and physical benefits. You may rise up faster and achieve more goals based on your autonomy, but you will be happier and healthier with a community of support. You will learn how to amass a team that honors who you are as a high achiever in chapter 7.

> *"When the day came that my boss told me I couldn't be promoted, I knew what my next exciting challenge would be . . . walking out the door and starting my own company. I'm a fast learner."*

> *"I rarely ask for advice. I'm sure I could use it, but I learned early on that I had to do things on my own if they were to get done. I'm not even a great team player. My behavior is so habitual I rarely notice when I put people off."*

What is the dark side of learning
the hard lessons at work?

- You are shocked by office politics and then only see the negative aspects of people's behavior instead of trying to understand what drives them to act the way they do. Your disillusionment keeps you from trying to work out differences. You would rather just leave even if you don't have a plan for where you will go next.
- You have difficulty recovering from being laid off, removed from a position, or placed in a position you don't want.
- You need reflection time to best understand what is going on within an organization. Because you love to stay busy, you may not get the quiet time you need to thoroughly think through complex situations.
- You may not seek or accept help and advice when offered. This could lead you to misread people's motives. You may learn from your mistakes, but you could avoid some of the problems if you accept guidance more often.

In short, you love proving to the world how amazing you are. You are worthy because of the extraordinarily impressive things you can accomplish. However, while you are in this whirlwind of achievement, taking charge, producing results and creating value, you may intimidate others, miss options, and regularly drive yourself to the point of exhaustion. Then you wonder if it is all worth it in the brief moments you take a breath. To help you feel positive and fulfilled, you will explore the darkest side of your high-achieving ways in the next chapter, "The Burden of Greatness." Then, in Parts II and III of this book, you will learn how to consciously choose the path you want to take for the rest of your amazing life.

TWO

The Burden of Greatness

The day the doctors told my father he could no longer work was the day he accepted his death sentence. If he had lived a long life and was terminally ill, maybe I could understand his death wish. He was only fifty-nine. He had gone deaf because of a growing brain tumor. The doctors said that the tumor was operable and that he might even be able to hear again. But they insisted he stop working. No matter how I tried to convince him that he still had a good life left to live, I failed. I wanted to shake him and tell him to stand up and fight as he had always taught me to do. The moment he sensed my anger, he rolled over and said he needed to sleep. The routine was the same every night for two weeks prior to his death.

In my anger for his leaving me, I somehow missed the lesson in my father's passing. My father could not be a retiree. He could not free himself from the identity of being a successful businessman. When he could no longer hold on to that identity, he quit. All he knew about life was to work hard, be the best, and help others achieve their dreams. He equated fun with achievement. He packed his "free time" with tasks, including being the president of every nonprofit group he belonged to. When he had to give up his formula for prestige, he gave up his will to survive. I desperately tried to help him see what else he could accomplish if he redefined his goals. I didn't see that his addiction to achievement was killing him.

It took me years to see that his legacy helped me to be wildly successful and almost killed me, too. I worked the night after his funeral, thinking that was what he would have wanted me to do. He wanted me to thrive, to succeed, and to show the world how great I was. I proceeded to be successful partly for myself and partly in honor of his dreams for me. Then one day, twenty years after his passing, I was sitting in the dark in my living room. I didn't have enough energy to turn on a light. I was forty-five years old. I owned a beautiful home plus the two cars in the garage. I had plaques and pictures demonstrating that I had achieved worldwide fame. In the dark, none of that was visible. There was something missing that kept me from enjoying my life. I was tired, unhappy, and had no idea who I was.

I WORK, THEREFORE I AM

The night I sat in my living room in the dark, I thought I was alone. I did not know that a growing number of women were just like me—confident, passionate, and successful, while also disillusioned, exhausted, and confused. We've been around for a while but only recently started showing up in research reports. With the best of intentions, our parents raised us to excel and our society persuaded us to achieve. Being ordinary was not an option. Yet being extraordinary is an elusive goal: there is always one more thing we can do before claiming the label. For every mountain we climb, there's another one on the horizon that must be conquered.

A 2006 study identified a number of ways women's work achievements are defining their identities.[1] This was a critical finding because in the past, studies generally found that women were much better than men at leaving their work persona at the office. Now, for most professional women, their work is their life. We have graduated from seeing work as something that will pay the bills to experiencing our careers as being an integral part of our identity. On the positive side, our skin is tougher than our predecessors. On the negative side, work has become all-consuming.[2]

The change in behavior of women at work after the mid-1980s is most profound among high-achieving women. The differences indicate both strengths and difficulties for today's top talent. What happened to cause this dramatic rift? Four societal shifts have been significant in rewiring the brains of women: the age of self-esteem, the increase in competitive sports for women, the push to earn advanced degrees, and the expectation of notable career success. I'll describe the shifts and then explore how, if taken to an extreme, the results can add up to being a deadly formula.

1. The Age of Self-Esteem

During the 1960s, a new word made it into our vocabulary: self-esteem. Although the word had been coined centuries before, it didn't become part of our social fabric until the 1960s and it wasn't seen as a must for children to have until the 1970s. Prior to this time, parents instructed their children to respect other people, especially their elders. Now self-respect comes first. We must love ourselves before we can love and respect others, or so we are told. Instead of trying to shore up our weaknesses, we should spend time discovering and celebrating the traits we have that can help us create a good life. As a result, many children who grew up during and after the 1960s in the United States and Europe have been taught to talk about "me." Self-absorption has become more than tolerated; it is expected.[3]

More importantly, the shift marked the first time in history girls were taught lessons in self-esteem. They were told they could do anything they wanted to do and be good at it. While boys have always been brought up to be independent and believe in their own strengths, girls had previously been socialized to rely on others. Now in progressive countries, young girls are not only seen and heard, but they are also told their opinions count. They are encouraged to question rules and challenge the status quo. Not only can they rise above the dependence of their mothers, but they can also make more money than their fathers. In fact, they can make about anything happen if they put their mind to it. The possibility of financial independence created an amazing shift in the mindset of young girls. Whether these possibilities would materialize when they became adults didn't matter. A girl's inherent right to success is solidified from childhood.

As if to make up for lost time, many girls are brought up not only to feel that they are strong and capable of achieving anything, but that they are exceptional and better than their peers.

> ***Beth, age thirty, said,*** *"I believe my parents think I can do no wrong . . . whatever I put my mind to in life, I achieved it if I wanted it. Whether it was making the volleyball team even after I got cut or getting the job with no experience. There's nothing that I want that I don't get."*

The women in my study all had one or more people in their lives, such as a parent, teacher, or sports coach, who told them they were special and that they could do anything. A survey participant said, "Looking back, I had an entire support system that acted as life cheerleaders encouraging me and my dreams. I still hear their voices when I face an obstacle. Then I remember that I am capable of achieving anything, even when other people back off." These voices go on long after the people are gone.

This socialization starts as girls are toddlers and continues throughout their schooling and into the workplace. Coloring books teach girls *It's All About Me* and *We Are All Special*, making "special" the new ordinary. In school, to be worthy they have to find what they can master, whether it is academics, sports, the arts, or all three. Liz Funk describes the dilemma of today's schoolgirls in her book *Supergirls*

Speak Out: Inside the Secret Crisis of Overachieving Girls.[4] She says the girls, including herself, take on the challenge to be extraordinary with a vengeance, constantly pushing themselves to the breaking point. As they become adults, Supergirls take their crusade into the workplace, where they look to rise above the crowd quickly and consistently.

> ***Kristi, age thirty-four, said,*** *"Being a garden-variety success is not good enough for me."*

We are brought up to believe that not only are we tough, but that we have to stand out and excel at something to be considered acceptable.

Today the media are full of strong female characters that appeal to both children and adults, enforcing the image that the exceptional female is the new norm. Books teach girls that they are special. The most popular television programs today feature strong, career-focused women. The women still seek love, but they don't give up their interesting and demanding careers for it. In the movie *Shrek*, the ogre's wife Fiona and her friends, Snow White, Cinderella, and Sleeping Beauty, are no longer damsels in distress. They are smart, independent, and capable of drop-kicking the bad guys. It's doubtful that lead female characters, live or animated, will ever be portrayed as dependent again.

As a result, we have a mentally strong generation of women with the upper end of the spectrum populated by more self-assured, dominant, and aggressive women than ever before. Even the most widely used measure of masculinity and femininity, the Bem Sex Role Inventory, has come into question owing to the changes in the attributes that women are showing. An increasing number of college-age women demonstrate qualities that used to define masculinity, such as being self-reliant, independent, able to defend one's beliefs, willing to take risks, and able to make decisions easily. However, these women also score high on traditionally feminine traits such as sociable, compassionate, understanding, and eager to work with others.[5] The results demonstrate that women aren't becoming more like men. They are becoming stronger as women.

These changes aren't happening just with American women. I teach programs around the world. In some countries, there may be only two or three women in a class who dare to talk to me about how they can have their voice heard more at work, but I've seen these numbers grow each year. Women are finding ways to use their energy and their abilities to their advantage. Women-owned businesses are increasing in China, Russia, and even Saudi Arabia. One of my clients in Russia told me, "Of course we are tough. Our men worked for Soviet companies for many years where they grew more and more passive. We women, on the other hand, were fighting over a loaf of bread. We are now taking that fight into the workplace." Super-confident, optimistic, open-minded, outspoken, and ambitious women are rising up everywhere they can.

2. *The Increase in Competitive Sports for Women*

Because of the acceptance and expansion of competitive sports for girls in the past forty years, many women can now fend for themselves physically as well as mentally. Even countries that tend to frown on women playing sports have both female athletes and sportscasters, an example being the Palestinian Territories, where Nelly Al-Masri has become a top sports journalist.[6] Each Olympics, more countries produce new female heroes. "Women hold up half the sky" and "Women can do what men can do" are not just popular slogans peddled by Chairman Mao; they have become reality for China's elite female athletes. In every Olympics since 1988, Chinese women have increased their representation over men. In other parts of the world, in addition to traditional women's sports such as gymnastics and swimming, sports such as soccer, golf, basketball, and track for women have become hugely popular among spectators as well as athletes. Whether training to be a world-class athlete or just enjoying a run through the neighborhood, women have found strength in their bodies as well as their minds.

> ***Ann, age fifty-two, said,*** *"Because of athletics I learned that even a small woman can be powerful. That feels pretty awesome when you were always the littlest in your class and you never grew past 5 feet tall. There's more to me than being cute."*

> ***Nancy, age forty, said,*** *"It was great for me to learn at an early age the joy of playing and competing and how to go home as friends at the end of the game."*

> ***Debbie, age forty-four, said,*** *"My family story is difficult, but my skating coach was exceptional in building my confidence."*

In the United States, this shift came in 1972 when the U.S. Congress passed Title IX, making it illegal for educational institutions receiving federal funds to bar anyone based on sex from attending a school program or activity. These activities included sports programs. The decision had football coaches shaking in their cleats. Coaches, teachers, and administrators jumped into action. The result—an impressive offering of women's competitive sports programs—blossomed in less than a decade. Even grade-school programs intensified. The increase of girls' sports has provided physical confidence and a sense of the power of teamwork. Both have helped women succeed in the corporate world.

3. The Increase in Women Holding Advanced Degrees

The academic muscle-building in women in the last two decades has been profound. American women earn 57 percent of the bachelor's degrees, 60 percent of all master's degrees, half of all professional degrees, and nearly half of all doctorates.[7] Many of these diplomas come from fields men used to dominate, from biology to business. "We're teaching girls that they need to be able to explore every opportunity that they are interested in," said Avis Jones-DeWeever, who oversees education policy for the Institute for Women's Policy Research.[8] According to the European Commission, women earn 43 percent of Europe's doctoral degrees in science.[9] Even in Iran, the number of young women earning university degrees is very high. More than half of the medical degrees in Tehran are earned by women.[10] Women's colleges are booming in countries such as Africa, Asia, and the Middle East where educating women is seen as a way to jump-start economic growth and political development.[11] In other countries, the Internet has allowed many women to circumvent the cultural restrictions that limit their physical access to schools and research. The increase in degrees gives women more career opportunities in addition to the ability to earn more money. Degrees not only open doors, but also give women the mental prowess to compete with men in the workplace.

4. The Expectation That Women Would Work and Be Good at It

All of this—the self-esteem movement, the rise in competitive sports for women, the increase in advanced degrees—is undermining the traditional expectations of women to settle down and become homemakers while promoting their success in a growing list of possible professions. In previous generations, if women worked, they didn't have to excel at it because they had a household to take care of. Now in countries that educate women, most high-achieving women enter the workplace with the expectation of creating a career, not just finding a job. They can open doors that used to say "Men Only," such as working in or owning construction and transportation businesses.

In fact, because women are now being told they should stand out among their peers, they expect to be recognized as outstanding performers in the workplace no matter what they choose to do. They are driven not to be good, but to shine above everyone else. Although they make frequent job changes and even career makeovers, they never lose sight of their power to excel. *As a result, today's strong, smart, and ambitious women know they can accomplish great things and they want to . . . over and over and over again.*

I BELIEVE I CAN FLY

In short, women are increasingly brought up to be self-sufficient not because they have to be but because they can be. They take their self-esteem with them into the workplace. They find career success early, often from the start. They often move into management positions within the first two years of working. At home, they have more support than previous generations, freeing them to focus on their careers. Many of my clients describe their husbands as actively supportive of their careers, not merely tolerant of them. The increase in household income also affords them nannies and housekeepers. In addition, in Western countries there has been an increase of women sharing responsibilities of both parenting and housekeeping with their mates. As a result, many of the internal conflicts and external pressures that women of previous generations faced are receding. Women now seem to face more career-oriented dilemmas, such as how long they should stay with one company or how to build a business of their own.

However, once women get a realistic sense of what they are capable of accomplishing in the workplace, they begin to question what they really want out of life. They can't quite pinpoint what makes them happy. They seek but can't define their ultimate purpose. They are being freed from old roles and customs without redefining who they are. They have no role models and no guidance to help them find their way. As a result, many high-achieving women bounce from job to job looking to find themselves, and fulfillment, in their work. They become wanderers hoping to stumble on the truth.

What could be a normal quest for self-improvement often turns into an obsession for discovering what is the absolute best accomplishment they can achieve. High-achieving women cannot rest until they can say, "I have done my best and it is enough." They have everything they were told would make them happy, but they are not. They are great at what they do, but there is always more to be done and greater challenges to be met. They seek purpose. They seek contentment. They are smart, confident, and assertive yet plagued by a restless agitation that keeps them from sitting still.

THE BURDEN OF GREATNESS

When artists create masterpieces and best-sellers, they feel an unrealistic expectation to repeat the miraculous. The same is true for many high-achieving women. They drive themselves crazy being excellent. Then, after spending little time enjoying their victories, they are back on track trying to repeat or even best their most outstanding performance. Because they can accomplish anything they put their mind to, this mental program is a never-ending loop.

The thought of having to be ordinary is terrifying. High achievers may never be able to accept a time when they can no longer be miracle workers. I was coaching a woman on the development of her speech we titled, "Life After Amazing." She had been a paramedic but had to quit at the ripe young age of thirty-four because of arthritis. She was struggling to find joy in her days where she wasn't saving lives under pressure. Working on the speech was laborious; she had not fully grieved the loss of her career. She had to let go of her dreams of being great in her chosen profession to see what other possibilities were available without feeling she had failed. Unfortunately, the abrupt end to my client's career broke her heart. She never called me again after our work together. My hope is that she found something else she could do that felt extraordinary.

I have come to call this phenomenon the "burden of greatness." Today's high achievers are brought up not only to be good, but also to believe they should be superstars at anything they choose to do. Because this goal is just as hard to define as it is to achieve, their restlessness rarely subsides. Even if they are aware of this phenomenon, they have to be continually alert to avoid succumbing to their overachieving habits, which tax their health and peace of mind.

This restlessness, along with the drive to excel, can cut them off from their feelings. They live in a frenzy of goals, chores, and to-do lists, barely conscious that their brains are telling them to keep moving if they are going to be worthy. They obsess about what they need to do differently in the future and in idle moments they play the "if only" game with the past. They are inclined to starve their natural need for love and connection while feeding their voracious appetite for new chances to excel. Sometimes they stop to catch their breath, but not for long. High-achieving women are wired to wander.

Yet there is hope for relieving the burden of greatness; there are ways to live in harmony with restlessness, making it a strategy instead of a quandary. One of my clients wanted to run from her successful law practice, claiming she wanted to teach literature instead. After we worked together for three months, she decided to find a partner for her practice so she could focus less on the operation of the business and more on litigation, which gave her the challenges she loved. Her decision also gave her more time to sit on a few boards in her community. She had hired me to help her stop and think about what she was doing, something she struggled to do for herself. Instead of escaping, she recreated who she is and what she does in a way that feels more fulfilling than obligatory.

MY FATHER'S DAUGHTER

My grandparents escaped to the United States from Russia when they were newlyweds, during the Bolshevik Revolution of 1917. My grandfather was fifteen and my grandmother was fourteen years old. They never saw their families again. It is likely that those who stayed behind were killed. They struggled in America, but they were alive. They raised five boys, my father being the oldest. My grandfather was often sick, but my grandmother found a good retail job and worked her way into management. She had the freedom to follow her beliefs and the opportunity to earn a good living. When I was young, I remember my grandmother jumping out of her chair in the middle of a conversation, throwing her right hand over her heart and declaring, "God bless America." Her depth of gratitude never ceased to amaze me.

Yet their own comfort wasn't enough; out of love, they expected their children to be educated and successful. Their offspring should make good money and provide well for their own families. They should have everything their hearts desired. For the most part, these dreams came true. The boys were all active in sports and excelled in their studies. When World War II broke out, the two older boys, including my father, left school to fight for their country. When they returned, they built successful businesses and reared families of their own. At my father's funeral, my uncle told me that my father wanted to be the family hero more than anything in the whole world. He was the oldest boy. His parents expected him to be the model son, which carried into his adult life. He worked hard at becoming a hero for his family and his growing community. I remember many people seeking my father's advice and money when I was growing up.

It wasn't until the funeral, when I heard my uncle talking about my father's intense need to excel, that I realized I was raised to live out my father's dreams. Of the four children in my family, I was the star athlete and student. I was definitely Daddy's girl. All I can remember about family gatherings is my father either talking about his growing business or his perfect children, especially me. Then he would have me recite a poem I had written or sing the last song I had memorized. I performed with panache. He beamed with pride. This legacy feeds my restless spirit even now. I'm not saying that he didn't love me just for myself, but I don't think he had any idea how heavy this burden would weigh on me as an adolescent and an adult.

My father's work ethic and expectations of grandeur were no less extreme than what had been passed on to my girlfriends by their parents. We girls were part of a group referred to as "the smart kids" or the "top-tier students." The kids who didn't excel in academics, sports, or the arts were second-rate. We were told to stay away from the second-rate kids. They just weren't good enough.

Therefore, I grew up having to excel in a "sea of excellers." I had to be the smartest, the best-looking, the most athletic, the most popular, the most creative, or even the funniest. And any combination of "bests" was even better. I do not recall being told to be the most compassionate, the most sensitive, the most generous (except to share with my little brother), the most peaceful, the most patient, the most accepting, or the most tolerant of my peers. I surely was never told to accept being second-best even if second-best was a great performance. Dinner conversations centered on what I had done well that day. Hungry for attention, I always found something to brag about. I never let on how hard it was to be the best when there were other very smart, very attractive, and very talented girls in my class.

When I reached adolescence, I rebelled against being "the best girl in the world," which led me to a path of drug abuse. It proved difficult for me to be the superstar in high school. There were hundreds more students to compete with. I was too short to excel in sports, and although I was acknowledged for my achievements in English and history, I struggled with the advanced courses in math and science that I needed if I wanted to have more than a "girly career." Worst of all, being a smart kid wasn't cool anymore. Because I couldn't keep up with what I thought my parents wanted for me, I looked to the most popular kids for recognition instead. The most popular kids spent their free time doing drugs. Because I was still driven to be the best, I couldn't be a mediocre drug user; I had to be the best drug user with the best drugs. Eventually I became hostile, self-destructive, and out of control. I can barely remember those years, or maybe I choose not to. I somehow still managed to complete my classes with high grades. My will to achieve stayed intact while my life crumbled around me.

I learned one of my greatest life lessons—if you don't know who you are, you will never be content with what you can do—in one of the darkest places on earth, a jail cell. A year after high school graduation, I ended up spending six months in jail for possession of narcotics, an experience I swore would never happen to me. In truth, the sentence saved my life.

In addition to stopping my negative spiral, I learned that scary strangers called inmates could be unexpected angels. In particular, the leader of the toughest gang decided I should be her friend. Vickie was a smart and vocal woman. She was also a mother and a daughter. I wrote poems for her to send to her family. She liked to play cards and I proved to be a great challenger. I think Vickie and I learned a lot from each other during the many nights we talked as we played cards until morning. I persuaded her to take the GED school course provided in the jail. She made me promise to write about her someday. Together, on my prompting, we staged a nonviolent protest, hoping to move to a larger cellblock because we had been locked down so many times for being overcrowded. When my idea failed and we ended up in an isolation cell, I declared my life to be one big failure. Vickie jumped at me, pinned me to the wall, and said, "You have no idea who you are, do you?

You're smart. You're strong. But for some God-knows-why reason, you care about people." She pointed to my heart. "When you can see what you are hiding in here . . ."—she then pointed beyond the bars—"you'll figure out how to be happy out there." That was my first lesson in understanding that "who I am" is different from "what I can accomplish." I didn't know who I was inside my shell of achievement. Even though I didn't fully understand her message at that moment, her words gave me the gumption to put my life back on track when I was released. I will never forget her words. I have been working on discovering and claiming my intrinsic value ever since. I will share specific exercises I have used in Part II of this book.

I went to college even more obsessed with proving myself because I now had a dark spot on my record to erase. Even more motivating was my sense that I had something important to do. If not for myself and my parents, I owed my future success to the women in jail who had taught me so much. I wasn't sure what I was going to do, but I knew I had the power to fight back. I graduated summa cum laude three years after my release from jail.

During my twenties and thirties, I willingly sacrificed my personal life and happiness for my work. I was unstoppable. Nothing could get in the way of my success, not even my marriage. My drive to be strong and to succeed left behind little room for love. I didn't develop any deep friendships and my marriage failed after five years. The psychologist Carl Jung described this journey best when he wrote, "Where the will to power is paramount, love is lacking."[12] The power I was thirsty for was based on my new drug of choice—achievement. I loved how it made me feel. Yet like cocaine, the high wore off fast and I needed more. At the age of forty, people saw my home, my cars, and my possessions and defined me as a successful, brilliant woman. They did not see that I was numb when working, I was bored when on vacation, and I barely existed beyond fatigue.

A LIGHT AT THE END OF THE TUNNEL

I have spent the last fifteen years waking up my senses. On a good day, I coach people on the phone while I sit in front of a big picture window where I can watch hawks circling the mountaintop and neighborhood cats chase each other up a tree. My clients tell me how I have changed their lives for the better and I remind myself that this is a big deal. I choose my work based on what I have defined as my purpose and say "no" to everything else. When I am buried under a to-do list, I prioritize and let some things go with no guilt. My exercise and fun time can't be compromised. These are the good days. I have to make decisions to live like this every day, sometimes every hour, so the old days don't creep back in.

In order to get some control over my life, I had to explore the dark side of my father's inheritance of excellence by asking myself some very difficult questions. When I find myself working too hard and filling in my free time by looking online for a new house, redesigning my Web site with a new focus, or dancing with the idea of starting a new line of business, I ask myself:

Who would I be if I were to stop everything and give voice to my heart? What have I imprisoned that wants to be free?
Would I cease to exist if I sat back and did the same work this year, even if I did it well?
Could I live feeling "ordinary"? Would this feel like giving up?
Is there a way to enjoy my restless rumblings without sacrificing love and peace of mind?

These questions, and others like them, have initiated powerful discussions for my clients as well as for me. Since I have begun my own search, I have worked with many female coaching clients who were also addicted to achievement. Together, we have been allowing our dark sides to see the light. In *Gone With the Wind*, Margaret Mitchell gave Rhett Butler a wise quote when he told Scarlett, "Until you've lost your reputation, you never realize what a burden it was or what freedom really is."[13] Since I have been asking myself the tough questions and researching the world of today's high-achieving women, I have found more specific ways of helping women appease their wanderlust and find true freedom, lessons I share in this book.

BECOMING WHOLE

If you recognize the Wander Woman in yourself, it is likely your gifts of intelligence, resourcefulness, courage, and determination have also been a burden. Some days you wonder if it is all worth it. You work hard. Your social life is pitiful. If you have children, you feel guilty for not spending more time with them. You hunger for a day of rest and long for a chance to pamper your body. You laugh when someone suggests you need life balance. The best you can do is balance your emotions as you go about your busy day. You can still love your friends, your partner, and your children, but you know there will always be an internal struggle about how you show your love.

This book is not about asking you to change who you are. I am asking you to better know who you are so you can have peace of mind. In this space of knowing, you will find the direction you've been seeking. You are extraordinary. You can still be brilliant and famous if you choose this path. You can channel your restlessness into creativity, exploration, and advocacy. Yet you can do this with a clear sense of direction and a full-hearted sense of contentment with yourself.

I am writing this chapter on an airplane, my office away from home. I can see the mountains that tell me we have crossed into my home state. I remember my grandmother jumping up and holding her hand over her heart as she thanked God for America. As a woman, she was learning what it felt like to be free to live out her dreams. Frankly, I think she would have been happy to see me be anything, as long as it was my choice, my whole-hearted and personal choice. It took me many years to reprogram my brain to clearly see what she and my father really wanted for me. I am honored to share these lessons with you.

PART II

Intentional Transformation

THREE

Claiming Your Selves

If you want to change how you relate to others and run your life, you have to first transform your concept of self. If you try to change your behavior without first transforming who you think you are, the changes will last a few days until you quit thinking about them. Then you will return to the same exhausting behaviors. Transformation is not a technical skill to be mastered. It is a process that includes identifying, reflecting, imagining, letting go, allowing things to unfold, and experimenting before you can step into the person you are most happy to be. The questions change from "What can I do?" to "Who can I be?" which takes some mental adjustment. The success you have created so far is built on what you brilliantly *do*. Now you have to define, refine and compose a new perception of who you *are* as you continue to perform.

THE WE THAT MAKES UP ME

One of the primary goals of coaching is to help you understand how your brain gives meaning to particular situations. Generally, you pay little attention to how you define the world around you as you go about your day. You have no knowledge that your brain is constantly scanning your environment, and then judging and explaining everything you see. This unconscious process enables you to act without having to think through every step. If you are working with a coach or someone adept in dialogue techniques, you can bring this process to light. You can explore the underlying beliefs that drive your behavior today, muse about what else is possible, speculate about the times you didn't act on an option, dream about the future, and, if you want to, accept a bigger reality for yourself. As you explore and expand your perception, you will come to know that you can alter your "selves-concept" to better achieve your goals.

I use the word "selves" when defining who you are because you are not uncovering your one true self; you are discovering the many faces you present. Because you move around a number of constantly evolving circumstances in your life, from work to home to hanging out with friends and family, your brain carries a library of selves. You call forth various aspects of your personality depending on where you are and who is present. All of these selves—the mixture that makes up who you are in the moment—are evolving along with the changes in your world and your life. So what is true for you today in any situation may shift for you tomorrow.[1]

You compose who you are based on what is needed from you at any particular time. You may have a core seed of self that doesn't change, but then you modify aspects of who you are in order to handle the situation you are facing. You usually do this unconsciously, with little control over the outcome. Through dialogue, reflection, and persistence you can increase your ability to adapt to circumstances by intentionally bringing forth different aspects of yourself for better results.

The process of expanding your sense of self—which includes the many selves you enact—can be called *intentional transformation* and is actually a method of rewiring your brain. As you learn and experience new things, you are continually rerouting and adding new synapses in your brain. According to the neuroscientist Joseph LeDoux, "Your synaptic connections hold the self together . . . there are always new connections waiting to be made."[2] *The speed of change then depends on how much you live in a state of curiosity instead of certainty.* The more open you are to considering new ways of thinking and acting, the faster the transmitters in your brain grow and expand. When you choose to see things from various points of view and shift how you feel about people and events, you intentionally change the structures in your mind. The point is—you don't find your identity; you expand your sense of self in your mind by learning, testing out new behaviors, reflecting on the results, and then repeating the process.

When you intentionally transform, you use both your imagination and your self-awareness. You look at who you are being today and what you feel is missing, and then you imagine a broader sense of self that will better serve your aspirations. Once you imagine yourself in a different light, you discover what skills and strengths you already have and then you determine the steps you need to take to fully integrate the new attributes. You mentally see who you want to be first. Then you create a plan for making this new version of you a reality.

One way of making this process more tangible is to work with archetypes. According to the work of Caroline Myss, archetypes are patterns of energy that you carry as you go about your life.[3] Some patterns are innate, wired into your brain when you are born. Other patterns take shape as you learn how to deal with difficulties and you are rewarded for specific behaviors. Archetypes can be defined as various aspects of your personality. However, they are not static traits. You not only act out these patterns in various situations, but you can also consciously call on specific aspects when you need them if you are aware of the various archetypes available to you.

The names given to the archetypes, such as Queen, Martyr, and Inspirer, are designed to help you identify a set of behaviors that might serve you or hurt you in a situation. For example, calling on your Queen archetype can be useful to you if you need to stand your ground when you are arguing for resources for your team. These same behaviors can be harmful if you play your Queen card when arguing with your spouse. Additionally, you can add certain archetypes to your repertoire through visioning and practice, such as adding the leadership energies of the Steward and the Collaborator, which are more *other*-focused than *I*-focused. We'll look at the most common archetypes for high-achieving women in this chapter. Working with your archetypes is a great way to facilitate your intentional transformation.

If you can identify the dominant and secondary archetypes present in your life right now, you will better understand the motivations for your actions and then choose new responses instead of acting habitually in various contexts. When you are running a meeting and it is not going well, you can call forth another archetype that might be more useful to you than the one that usually dominates. On the other hand, if you understand how the archetypes you are expressing serve your higher purpose, you can better articulate why you choose to behave in a certain way even when others disapprove, such as when you feel that your obsessive behavior is necessary in order to meet a deadline.

Because archetypal patterns are not roles but names you give to the patterns of behavior you are expressing, they show up differently in people, so you will want to test out various options for yourself. As your wisdom grows with maturity, you will release old patterns of behavior. Other patterns will gain dominance that better help you overcome roadblocks and reach your new goals. For example, I called on Warrior energy early in my career to help me fight my way up the ladder in two male-dominated corporations. Now I gain better results when I call on Connector and Inspirer energies. Over time, my Connector and Inspirer began to show up more than my Warrior, though all three are still aspects of who I am. You will naturally repeat new behavioral patterns that are rewarded, making them more central to your personality. This process of identifying, focusing on some, and decreasing other behavioral patterns is how you change who you are so that the changes you make last over time.

An archetype should not be used as a label to stereotype yourself or others. Stereotypes are judgments based on how you see people fall in or out of your cultural and personal norms. You stereotype women when you label the first generation of managers Queen Bees and Bully Broads. I've heard some people refer to today's high-achieving women as Princesses and Lone Wolves. If you label a woman, you then relate to her as if her identity is defined only by these names. A label reduces a person to one description whether or not she is acting that way in the moment. This makes it difficult for you or anyone else to step out of the stereotype and try on new behaviors. If you want to feel supported as you explore different identities, avoid seeing anyone as a stereotype. When you see the many aspects all people express, you increase not only your capacity to recognize multidimensionality in others but also your ability to accept the many aspects of yourself. The names given to the archetypes are identifiers so you can articulate and work with the energy patterns. No *one* archetype could possibly represent who you are as a human being.

THE VOICES IN YOUR HEAD

The following archetypes are the most common in the high-achieving women I have coached, but represent only some of the patterns you may express. I worked out the descriptions with Jim Curtan, who teaches workshops and coaches people to expand their personal awareness and development using archetypes.[4] If you are interested in a more comprehensive list with descriptions, I recommend the book *Sacred Contracts* by Caroline Myss and its companion, *Archetype Cards and Guidebook*, to visually lay out your archetypes to see how they interrelate and conflict. She provides blank cards for you to add in your own archetypes if you don't see ones that characterize a special aspect of your personality.

You start your life with immature patterns and then expand your repertoire as you mature. Everyone is born with the Victim, Prostitute, and Saboteur archetypes.[5] For example, when you were young, you lacked a sense of personal responsibility. If you didn't get what you wanted, you blamed the source of your unhappiness on others as you played out the energy of the Victim. Typically adolescents act with the energy of the Prostitute when they give away what should be dear to them, such as their bodies, time, love, and health. The Saboteur shows up when you aren't clear about what you really want in life and then find yourself trapped in a situation that feels uncomfortable or wrong for you. If you don't have the courage to face the truth and move on, you unconsciously summon your Saboteur to damage the relationship, project, or career. Personal growth often focuses on decreasing the energies of the Victim, the Saboteur, and the Prostitute. New, more powerful archetypes emerge as you mature that are more instrumental in achieving your goals, such as the Visionary, the Revolutionary, and the Magician. Once you define your most powerful archetypes and consciously call on them to help you resolve difficulties, your Victim, Prostitute, and Saboteur will retreat. Unfortunately, they never fully disappear. You may strive to be perfect, but these energies remind you that you are human. Here's how these three archetypes show up as adults.

The Victim. When you express the Victim, you refuse to take responsibility for your difficulties and instead blame others. This archetype is commonly seen in organizations when employees blame difficult situations on a colleague, the boss, or "the bureaucracy/corporation." As the Victim, you focus on what you can't control. A little venting may be healing, but expressing too much Victim energy can be depressing. As a high achiever, you are rarely a Victim and you don't like being around people who thrive on this energy.

However, everyone whines now and then. The Victim may show up when you are fatigued or disappointed.

The Saboteur. If there is a fear of failure or a fear of success, the Saboteur steps in to protect you from either scenario. This archetype is often active in women with an Imposter complex. They unwittingly make sure a project or relationship fails before it becomes evident that they aren't capable of succeeding. As a more confident high achiever, you probably aren't afraid of success. Instead, you might sabotage your goals if there is any possibility that you might fail. You cope with setbacks far better than outright failures, so you avoid what appears to you to be high-risk activities. Be aware of how you rationalize your behavior when you refuse to do something. Your Saboteur may be leading you to exaggerate the downside.

The Prostitute. When you do not ask for enough compensation or you constantly give more time and energy to projects than was expected, you are expressing the Prostitute archetype. Prostitutes struggle with saying "no." When your need to be regarded as the star keeps you from setting stringent boundaries, you give yourself away too easily. In the end, you burn yourself out or hold resentment for the people who took you up on your offers.

Two more significant archetypes are the Wanderer and the Pioneer. The distinction between these two is important. The Wanderer is one of your dominant archetypes. At times you may also call forth the Pioneer if you like to do things no one in your family, company, or community has done before. If you have a passion for being "first" and your vision for this goal is clear, you are also a Pioneer. However, Wanderers rarely become Settlers as many Pioneers do.

The Wanderer seeks new opportunities and freedom. When you act with this pattern of energy, you accomplish many things because of your constant desire to move forward, even though ultimately you aren't sure where you are going. You tend to base your career decisions more on present needs than on a long-term vision. If you don't like what is going on, you move on to the next opportunity. You trust you will land on your feet. However, you can also lose your sense of self in the process of constantly leaving. Your need to wander may become compulsive, never allowing you to settle down and be still.

The Pioneer seeks new territories and opportunities. You tend to be different from the people in the new job or community, either physically or mentally. As a Pioneer, you have a specific mission that drives your decisions. You also have a clear vision of what you want to manifest. You may become a Settler when you find a company or a community that will allow you to carry out your plans.

The following archetypes represent patterns that may be dominant in your life right now or more latent archetypes you would like to bring forward. Some will feel familiar to you. You can easily see how their characteristics fit into your self-concept. Others will feel foreign to you and may never be relevant for you. After you read each description, assign the archetype a number on a scale of 1 to 10 where 10 suggests a pattern that you frequently play out and 1 doesn't reflect you at all. If the description resonates with a part of your nature you would like to demonstrate more often, score the archetype as a 5 or above. In the next chapter you will learn how to integrate archetypes you would like to express more often. With trial and reflection, you will be able to compose a new sense of self that supports the changes you want to make.

Following the descriptions of common archetypes for high-achieving women, you will find a more comprehensive chart that includes the names of other patterns you might resonate with. Use this table as an index when you want to quickly refer to and compare the patterns. I will then give you exercises to help you determine your dominant and secondary archetypes and how you can use them to achieve your goals.

The Adventurer. You are the idea person. You love coming up with creative answers to recurring problems. All it takes is someone to describe a situation in a few sentences and you can't wait to share the perfect solution you discovered. Once you find the answer, unless the solution requires your unique expertise, you quickly switch your attention to the next dilemma to be solved. You don't like working on one project for very long. People like to be around you because you have a positive outlook and you embrace the many joys and wonders of life, including new technologies and progressive methods. You also frustrate people because they can't always tell when you've moved on to something new. *Score 1–10* ______

The Coach. When you trust that people you are helping are capable of finding their own way even when they aren't so sure of themselves, you take on the Coach archetype. You become a "thinking partner" instead of a Teacher or Mentor who provides solutions. You are curious and more interested in what people have to say than in telling them what to do. You ask good questions, reflect on what you hear, encourage others to try out ideas, and support them when they do. The Coach exercises patience. If you aren't a patient person, be careful when calling on your Coach. If you get frustrated when people don't come up with answers as quickly as you would like, you might jump in and use a more directive pattern that could ruin the trust you built. *Score 1–10* ______

The Detective. You have great powers of observation. You see details others often miss. You have a thirst for knowing more, for learning, and for seeking the truth. Like the Coach, you are naturally curious, which makes you a good listener with solid intuition. However, you also tend

to be naturally skeptical and doubt people before you trust them. If you want to create a trusting bond with someone, you may have to accept what you see on the surface.
Score 1–10 ______

The Magician. Based on your many experiences, you can see through illusions and achieve grand things that others could not conceive. You like making things happen even if you have to do them yourself. Successful entrepreneurs are Magicians. You optimistically believe in possibilities. You believe that if one door closes, another one will soon open. *Score 1–10* ______

The Queen. If you sense that you must rule a kingdom of people, whether it's your family or work group, you carry the energy of the Queen. You like to make decisions and you are comfortable with the power you have for getting others to implement what you decide. If you like to make sure everyone below you is taken care of and happy, you will be seen as a compassionate Queen. If you don't demonstrate concern when you declare your decisions, you will be perceived as self-serving and your followers will resent your authority. Even if you reject the notion that you act as a monarch, if you walk into a room as if you own it, you probably carry the energy of the Queen. *Score 1–10* ______

The Rebel. If you reject both conformity and authority, you carry the energy of the Rebel. Rebel energy is needed when traditional systems are strongly set in place and transformation is past due. When the Rebel dominates, you may stubbornly hold your ground, rejecting even legitimate authority and traditions. You may lose perspective when you are deep in your rebellion. You also miss opportunities for aligning with others if all you see is a power struggle.
Score 1–10 ______

The Revolutionary. Whereas Rebels break down old structures, Revolutionaries build new ones. To be a Revolutionary you need a clear vision of the grand changes you want to bring about. Even if the changes you envision

will take years to come to pass, your vision keeps you going. You are willing to challenge the status quo to make your vision a reality. However, if you do not earn the respect of your colleagues, you will be seen as a Rebel.
Score 1–10 ______

The Storyteller. You love to be the center of attention. You captivate your audiences with life stories that help them learn something about themselves. All experiences provide good material for your metaphoric lessons. Sometimes your stories are out of place so you need to be sure your audience is open to gaining the wisdom you want to impart. If not, you will look more out-of-touch than wise.
Score 1–10 ______

The Superstar. You love being the top performer, whether in the workplace, the classroom, or on the sports field. You have to stand out. You don't care to share the limelight. In meetings, you like being the one with either the right or most creative answer. You seek acknowledgment, even fame, for your outstanding work. You are gracious to others and may even be a good Teacher as long as no one questions your ideas. People may pay you good money to perform. The more visible you are, the easier it is to get work. On the other hand, you may struggle with being a team player if the environment is collaborative. In general, it will be hard for you to find contentment at work and in life when you aren't being the Superstar. Maintaining this status can be exhausting and, in the end, unfulfilling. *Score 1–10* ______

The Teacher. If you love to share all the wisdom you gather as you wander, the Teacher archetype will give you both a sense of purpose and a source of joy. You easily synthesize diverse ideas and translate them in a way that your audience can understand. However, you are offended when your teachings are rejected or challenged. Your Warrior may emerge if you defend your point of view and fuel the conflict. You then miss the chance to learn something new.
Score 1–10 ______

The Thinker. You have learned to watch with keen eyes before you speak. You prepare your presentations carefully, knowing you are right about your conclusions. Sometimes, you rock the world with your amazing, well-researched ideas. People then seek your wisdom. Other times, your attention to detail is too limiting. You are sensitive to criticism because you have worked hard to be right. You have a hard time accepting other people's perspectives if they differ from your own because you feel you are the most capable person in the room. If you have a strong academic background, you may also call on the Scholar archetype when making your theoretical arguments. *Score 1–10* ______

The Warrior. You use your strength, skill, and discipline to fight for the rights of others, hoping to make your company, home, or community a better place to live. Although you like to be on the offense where you are moving mountains to create change, you are ready to defend yourself at a moment's notice. You staunchly protect and fight for your rights. You may even enjoy a good fight, which shuts other people down. When your passion becomes angry, you might overuse your Warrior strength and become a Bully who damages her relationships. When you're stressed and people question your motives, you may verbally cut off their heads with your brash responses. People will then avoid giving you feedback, so you will not get the information you need to make the best decisions. *Score 1–10* ______

Common leadership archetypes include:[6]

The Collaborator. As a Collaborator, you take an active role in making sure there is full participation by all parties involved. Instead of speaking to audiences, you build and work with communities. You act as a partner who is willing to make the time to listen and understand all points of view. Everyone's voice must be heard. You have the ability to see the big picture so you know how to fold everyone's needs and ideas into team solutions. Some people will marvel at your patience. Others will see your actions as a waste of time, wishing you were more decisive. *Score 1–10* ______

The Commander. When you act as the Commander, you accomplish a lot but you often appear as a Taskmaster because you prioritize rules and goals over the needs of people. As a high achiever, you hold others to your own high standards and you revert to Commander patterns when you think people are falling behind. At times taking command is vital. At other times this energy will damage morale and relationships, so you want to listen and coach instead of command. Commander energy should be used in limited quantities. Carefully choose when you want to express this energy instead of habitually using it as a fallback pattern. *Score 1–10* ______

The Connector. When you introduce and weave together the tasks of people from different perspectives and backgrounds, you are calling on the Connector. You may use many communication platforms to give people the opportunity to connect and create results together, including social media. Connectors have a lot of tools to work with in this age of the Internet. *Score 1–10* ______

The Heroine. On your personal journey, being the Heroine will help you stay the course of growth as you tackle obstacles and wrestle inner demons. As a leader, you call on the Heroine when you need to take calculated risks to help your team. You lay out the plan and then courageously fight the battles with upper management to help smooth the way for change. Sometimes you overuse the Heroine and fix things more for the recognition of your heroics than for the results. This showboating can annoy people over time. Also, if you want to develop other people on your team, being their Heroine and solving problems for them can hinder their growth. Let other people be Heroes and Heroines, too. Coach them on how to strategize, gamble on the odds, manage conflicts, and solve problems as you have learned to do. Call on the Steward and Inspirer patterns to help you nurture a heroic team. *Score 1–10* ______

The Inspirer. You are able to articulate a compelling vision. Then, instead of using threats, you prompt people into action by helping them feel they can be significant in achieving the vision. When you call on the Inspirer, you use active listening in addition to profound and encouraging language to rouse people into dedicated action. People who feel inspired by your words and your vision put extra effort into their work because they want to, not out of obligation or fear. *Score 1–10* ______

The Steward. When you help others to understand their talents, strengths, and potential and then support them as they work you are a Steward leader. You put the service of others before yourself. The environment you create is safe for people to make personal discoveries and to experiment with what they learn. You allow people to learn from their mistakes. When you feel your greatest achievements are found in the success of others, you are calling forth the Steward. *Score 1–10* ______

The Visionary. You use stories and pictures to help others see possibilities beyond what is happening today. You have the ability to envision what others can't yet see. You are good at offering hope in difficult times. In some situations you will have to quit talking and either start working or delegate tasks to others to make sure long-term goals are completed. If you also carry Adventurer energy, you will get bored easily with routine tasks and may forget the details of your promises. Make sure systems are in place to track your commitments. *Score 1–10* ______

• •

✓ **EXERCISE:** Choosing Your Board of Directors

When you look at the narrative of your life, what characters do you see yourself playing?

STEP 1

Using your scores, select your top ten dominant selves from the following list. If you struggle with choosing, ask someone who knows you well to help you limit your list to ten. Some of the archetypes in this list weren't described but may be highly relevant for you, so consider circling them as well.

Victim
Wanderer
Warrior
Thinker
Commander
Inspirer
Martyr
Taskmaster
Entertainer
Comedian
Detective
Scholar
Idealist
Prostitute
Pioneer
Revolutionary
Adventurer
Steward
Heroine
Advocate
Coach
Mentor
Magician
Connector
Companion
Artist
Saboteur
Queen
Rebel
Storyteller
Visionary
Collaborator
Superstar
Healer
Mother
Teacher
Bully
Femme Fatale
Gambler

STEP 2

Choose six of the archetypes you circled that you express most often right now in your life. These six archetypes are the Board of Directors making your life decisions. Bring them together in one place and you can be Chairman of the Board. Naming your archetypes gives you more control over your behavior. The more quickly you identify when you are calling on one archetype, the sooner you can choose to call on another one if you think the results will be better.

• • • •

EXPLORING YOUR ARCHETYPES

Being aware of your behavioral patterns requires you to stop and evaluate your reactions in the moment. You need to sense and quiet your impulses before you can try out a different response. For example, if you are a Teacher and a student challenges you, whether this student is an employee, your child, or a friend, you might quiet the Teacher and consider what other patterns would better achieve your goals. Even though you are standing at the front of the room, the Teacher may not be the best archetype to use to help people gain a new perception in a conflict situation. Once you are free to choose, you can call on the Seeker to stimulate your curiosity, the Coach to ask questions, and the Collaborator to see the bigger picture and blend differing perceptions into a common goal. To make this shift, first recognize the patterns of energy that are aroused. Then remind yourself what you are trying to accomplish. With your goals in mind, choose other energies that would be more useful to you in the moment.

• •

✎ **EXERCISE**: Your Circle of Selves

Taking the six archetypes you chose as your Board of Directors, write each title on a small square of paper or Post-it® note. Choose the archetype you think is your dominant pattern, the behavior you fall back on when under pressure. Place this one in the middle and lay out the other five archetypes around it. Add two or three archetypes to the circle that you feel are a part of your nature but you haven't expressed much. Reflect on what you have laid out. Write down your insights. Review your Circle of Selves at least once a day for the next week and then again monthly to support your transformation.

• • • •

When you understand what drives your behavior based on your dominant archetypes, you can choose to play out your other patterns to save your relationships. For example, as a Queen, you naturally put your kingdom and your mission before your personal relationships. If other people in your life understand that you have a strong commitment to serving the common good, they will accept supportive positions. If not, your loved ones will feel abandoned or disrespected. Either way, you occasionally need to step down to let your loved ones share the throne. Call on your Companion or Steward archetype to soften your Queen.

If you identify with the Rebel, consider calling on the Revolutionary instead, especially if you are trying to change a system instead of just defying it. Rebels may win battles, but Revolutionaries win the war. If you serve your mission and not your ego, you can help an organization or group transform. Every executive team should have a strong and respected Revolutionary in their midst. To be a successful Revolutionary, you need to speak using the language of your peers so everyone involved understands what you envision and why. Otherwise you will be pegged a contrarian Rebel or an Idealist who doesn't have a clue about what is going on. If you want to have a lasting impact on a system, call on the energies of the Visionary and the Inspirer to persuade people to embrace your ideas.

• •

EXERCISE: Using Archetypes to Manage Difficult Conversations

The next time you find yourself in conflict with someone or you are struggling to present your ideas in a way that will be heard, ask yourself these two questions:

What archetype am I speaking with right now?
What other archetype would I like to express to resolve this conflict effectively?

• • • •

Before you can control the world around you, you must first master your thoughts and behaviors. Mastery starts with clarifying and expanding your self-concept. Be honest when identifying what archetypes you express, including the dark as well as light sides of each. If you struggle with this, you can find a coach to work with who is versed in using archetypes.[7] Using archetypes gives you a concrete way to talk about who you are and who you want to be.

BALANCING YOUR ENERGIES

Once you identify your dominant archetypes and the ones you would like to develop, the goal is to balance your energies so one does not take over and become a tyrant. You may appreciate being a Wanderer. Yet the fulfillment you seek could come with developing your Visionary, Artist, and Mentor energies. Also, your restlessness may keep you from falling into ruts, but you are frustrated when new people fail to recognize your value when they meet you. You may need to call forth your Collaborator to discover how your skills can match up with their needs so they more quickly see your value. You may lose sight of the bigger picture as a Warrior or Rebel and keep fighting after you have won the battle. Call on your Thinker or Detective to better analyze what how much force you need to wield. Keeping your archetypes in balance is a special practice. Peace of mind comes with having a well-balanced array of archetypes.

• •

EXERCISE: Balancing Archetypes

To help balance the energy of your archetypes, ask yourself the following questions:

Who would I be if I didn't need to complete all the tasks on my lists? Is there another archetype calling me that I've been too busy to hear?

When I look at my calendar, which of my archetypes would best serve me today?

What would relieve my frustration and anger? Could seeing through the lens of a different archetype give me the perspective I'm missing?

What if my computer didn't work today and I had to stay in my office . . . what would I do? What archetype could I call on to help pass the time?

• • • •

LEADING AS A WAY OF BEING

As a high achiever, the archetypes you call on to be seen as smart, resourceful, and creative can stand in the way of your ability to inspire others to be their best. Whether you have a formal title or not, you may hold a position where others look to you to provide leadership. You have to judge when it's best to let go of performing so you can lead. When you are being the best performer, you distance yourself from the people you are supposed to be guiding. Although you may logically know his, your ego will make it hard for you to let go of the identity associated with the archetypes of personal accomplishment. For example, if you are usually the smartest one, the Scholar, on your team, it will be hard for you to let others think they know something you don't. Yet great leaders ask for help from their team members and accept ideas that are different from their own. Call on your Coach energy to use questioning to help others discover the truth for themselves. If you were the top salesperson because you are a courageous Heroine and a Gambler who trusts her intuition to take risks, it's probably hard for you to stand back and let others make decisions. Call on your Steward and Teacher energy to help your team members assess situations and take action on their own. If you think you were hired to make tough bottom-line decisions, then you might see yourself as the Commander. You still have to be the Inspirer to motivate people to follow you and be the Visionary to align their energies around a compelling picture of the future.

If you can't flex your self-concept, you will either fail as a leader or you will choose to move on to another job or career where you can staunchly defend the glory of who you think you authentically are. On the surface, your decision to leave might look like you are being true to yourself. You feel underappreciated and misunderstood. Ask yourself if your Rebel or Warrior is keeping you from trying on new behaviors, making you feel that you are giving in if you change. If you jump ship at this point, you might be leaving behind a chance to expand your range of skills and capabilities. Your inflexibility stunts your growth. You can never go from being a great achiever to a being a memorable leader without quieting your old dominant voices so you can hear what your other archetypes have to say.

Management training and leadership books tell you what types of behaviors work best, but you will not take on these behaviors until you alter the framework of *who you are*. Being a leader means more than learning new skills. I was coaching a district sales manager who was struggling with getting her team to complete their administrative tasks. She said she felt forced to act like a policewoman having to remind them to obey the rules. She asked me what she could do differently to make them comply. Instead of brainstorming approaches, I asked her to define herself as a leader. Her answer focused on carrying out the responsibilities of the company. She said she was tasked with seeing that her district met their sales goals and that her team never showed up on any lists for not completing company directives.

I told her that her job description felt like she held the identity of Taskmaster. No wonder her employees resisted her whip. She angrily corrected me, telling me how deeply she cared about them and their successes. She wanted to help them enjoy their jobs and be proud of their individual wins as much as she wanted them to reach their sales goals.

She resented that anyone would think she was solely driven by results. Yet when I asked her for examples of how she demonstrated her devotion to her team, all she could tell me was that she provided quick follow-up when her employees made requests. I interviewed her direct reports. It was no surprise that they described her as overwhelming in her demands and patronizing in her tone. They felt she was more invested in demonstrating her expertise than in trusting and developing theirs. She never spent time listening to them; she didn't get to know who they were and what they needed. If they came to her with a concern, she was quick to jump in with solutions instead of coaching them to find their own. They were afraid to give her feedback. Not that they thought she was a bad person and would hurt them, but because she obviously didn't trust them, they couldn't trust her. I could have told her to back off and quit micromanaging. I could have taught her coaching skills. I could have worked with her on specific scenarios and helped her find new solutions. Yet I didn't want to waste our time.

Before she could behave differently, she had to see herself in a new light. This was not an easy process for her. It took suppressing some old familiar voices as well as taking the risk to be someone new with her team. She wasn't sure that the shift would help her professionally. Although the organization professed to honor human values, these came second to goals that increased the bottom line. She received little support from her own manager for anything that didn't directly involve hitting the sales goals. She might have remained on a decent career path in spite of her team's discontent because their sales numbers were good. However, my client's incentive was more personal than professional. She truly cared about her team members and she was exhausted by the current scenario, so she chose to brave the journey of intentional transformation. She committed to change her self-concept in this context, which would in turn change her style. I'll explain the steps she took in the next section.

COMPOSING A LEADER

The transformation process takes time. Once you identify how you want to balance your energies, you cannot "change" your self-concept as you would a piece of clothing. In the same vein, you cannot write a vision describing the new you and just set goals to achieve it. The process is dynamic and nonlinear. It takes place by reflecting on events that are happening or recently completed and then imagining different ways of being in those situations. Once you can see how different behaviors will better serve your ultimate goals, you can use visioning to create a picture of how you will fully express yourself as the new you. The vision becomes your map, helping to guide you when you stop and make choices about how you want to be perceived. Visioning will also help you clearly articulate your intentions and commitments. I'll give you a method for doing this type of visioning in chapter 4. In chapter 7, you will learn techniques for making sure you stay with the process long enough for the transformation to take hold.

Getting back to my client: we started the transformation process by exploring how she defined her current identity as a leader and, more important, how she could see herself in other ways that would be more effective with her team. We explored how the Commander archetype and her mission *to get things done* caused resistance in her team. She listed everything she thought was true about the people she managed, including their laziness and lack of commitment, and then brainstormed other possible "truths" for their current behavior. After looking at her team from a new perspective, she restated her mission. Instead of being the leader who made sure things got done, she wanted to be a leader who *inspires others to get things done*. We then explored the archetype of the Inspirer. This led her to imagine new ways of acting and reacting when communicating with her team. As a result, she daily tested out new thought patterns and behaviors and let go of old ones. Over time, she could see herself changing—thought by thought and action by action.

• •

✎ **EXERCISE:** Composing Your Self

1. In five words or less, define yourself by the mission you have been trying to accomplish, not by your role or tasks.
2. Based on this mission, how do you expect people you associate with to behave? Name the archetype that describes the behavior you most often portray.
3. What stories are you telling about the people you are dealing with? Could they be telling these stories differently?
4. What is most important to you about this situation? What do you fear? What do you passionately believe?
5. What do you like about yourself right now? What doesn't feel so good?
6. What mission would you like to have going forward?
7. Name the archetype(s) you would like to bring in to help you accomplish your mission.
8. How can you balance these new archetypal energies with your energies that tend to dominate? What can you do to honor your new self-concept?

Spend time on each question. Write about it, talk about it, sleep on it, and see if you wake up with a new idea. Intentional transformation first requires you clearly see what you are releasing. From this vantage point, you can then see who else you can be. Once you learn how to shift your self-concept on your own, you will never again feel stuck when searching for changes you can make to improve a situation.

• • • •

THE BUST OF WANDERLUST?

On a final note, please don't think I'm suggesting you stop being a Wanderer. I'm saying that if you are facing a frustrating situation, there are other strengths and energies you can call on for better results. You can balance your Wanderer energy with patterns that will help you improve your relationships, clarify your direction, and find the contentment you seek. If you are happy with the full sense of who you are—including all facets of your being—you can stand just as tall in any setting as you can walk tall out the door. Define yourself holistically. You can then consider many options before leaping onto another path.

FOUR

Debunking Your Assumptions

Disclaimer: This chapter is "R" rated for reality.
If you aren't ready to face some hard truths about your beliefs you may want to block this chapter from viewing.
HOWEVER, if you are serious about feeling happier with your work and more peaceful about your future . . .

I believe there is a common misunderstanding around the definition of the word *perfectionist.* The people who work with me will tell you I'm an annoying perfectionist. I don't agree. I'm not a fan of details. My accessories don't always match. I would rather complete a project and get it out the door than fall asleep at my desk reviewing it one more time. However, my computer's thesaurus says you can substitute the words "uncompromising," "stickler," and "someone who likes to do things properly" for "perfectionist." Because I tend to be the one defining what "properly" is and it takes a major dose of willpower for me to let someone do something differently than I would, then you might call me a perfectionist. When it comes to doing something important to me, I'm an uncompromising stickler about how I think things should be done. Perfectionists aren't just people preoccupied with details, order, and efficiency. High achievers as uncompromising sticklers are performance perfectionists.

You didn't find Perfectionist on the archetype chart because it represents a mindset that acts as the container for all the archetypes you express. For you, Wander Woman, "perfectionist" is more of a paradigm than a pattern. A paradigm is a framework that represents a specific way of organizing and interpreting reality. When you refuse to see things differently, you are "thinking within the box" of your paradigm. However, in order to change your thoughts and behaviors, including how you use your archetypes, you have to break down the walls of your box.

Your paradigm of perfection is held together by three assumptions you have that are explained in this chapter. These assumptions have helped you to be amazing. They serve you professionally in many ways that make you appear more successful than most people. However, they also keep you from personally growing. Even though they have served you in the past, you must find fault with these three assumptions in order to crack the walls of your paradigm enough to allow yourself to change. After you explore the assumptions, you will be given directions for visioning your life with a new set of beliefs. You will create your vision of yourself as excellent but imperfect using the archetypes you chose in the last chapter. You will also be given an exercise to develop keywords you can use to recall your visions when you most need them.

Whether or not you think of yourself as a perfectionist, if you put an intense amount of energy into creating amazing results, you will find it difficult to feel content with anything. Even at the pinnacle of your career, you will sense there is something missing. "When I got to this destination called 'success,' it wasn't what I thought it should be," said Carol Mann, one of the most successful female golfers in the 1960s and 1970s and a member of the LPGA Hall of Fame. She asked, "Is this all the accomplishment I can expect? Do I have to keep doing this?"[1] When you experience this emptiness, your tendency as a Wander Woman is to search for what else you can do to feel fulfilled. I had breakfast with a woman who went from being a celebrated marine biologist to an international sales executive to a management consultant and is currently on the boards of several performing arts organizations in a major city while raising her daughter and contemplating her next career move. When I asked her if she was a perfectionist, she laughed, shook her head "no," and said, "I'm passionate, not perfect." She went on to tell me that she also earned three degrees from Stanford, crossing over from biology to business. I asked her if her path had brought her happiness; she said she is only now stopping to ask herself that question. She was taught to raise her hand first and give the best and brightest answers. *For the first time in her life, she is questioning what she is raising her hand for.* Her passion brought her great success, but she couldn't say that it had brought her contentment.

On the road of perfection, feeling happy and having fun with others while working are also elusive concepts. You probably feel numb more than any specific emotion because that is how the mind copes with incessant stress.[2] Over time, you learn to repress the expression of your emotions to survive, which also has a negative effect on your emotional and bodily functions.[3] When you shift into "working mode" you unconsciously teach your brain that your feelings are not useful to your survival. The neuropathways to this center then shrink in size, limiting your ability both to feel your own emotions and to empathize with others.[4] In other words, the more you suppress your feelings to get your work done, the less you are able to feel happiness and to connect emotionally with your colleagues. You biologically become joyless and inadvertently become insensitive.

Besides losing the capacity to feel joy, a more harmful side effect of suppressing your emotions is that the feelings you hold back are eventually released on unsuspecting targets. You don't stop the anger and frustration; you hold the sensations in until you can't take it any longer, raging in traffic, insulting your spouse, and making your colleagues wrong for minor matters. This is when they label you Bossy. When I reach the end of my rope, I become a "head biter."

My patience disappears and I snap at people who interrupt me by phone or knock on my door. Other signs of being flooded by stress are the use of sarcasm, micromanaging, second-guessing decisions, interrupting, abruptly ending conversations, and forgetting to be courteous to people who are just doing their jobs. The less happy and content you feel, the more impatient you are.

At times when you strive to be the Collaborator and the Inspirer, it will be easy for you to forget your intentions when the pressure rises. If you are always right, you won't give in to any argument. If you can't be the Superstar, you sit back and detach from the process. Because everyone knows you get good results, they find a way to work around you instead of with you. They may highly regard your intelligence and ability. At the same time, they view your string of outstanding results with envy and possibly disdain. You may be surprised when someone has the guts to tell you that you intimidate others because you view yourself as socially adept, but it is your actions more than your demeanor that separates you. *Your chronic need to get it right and be the best keeps you separate.*

You need to feel that connection and contentment are worth the time and effort you will have to give to changing how you think and act. Otherwise, you will have little tolerance for the uncertainty and messiness of personal transformation. When you choose to take on a new identity, you may stumble for a while and feel you aren't progressing. There may be a period of time when you can't control the outcome. Therefore, before you attempt to apply what you learn in this book, you must accept that your transformation is one goal you can't do perfectly.

It takes courage, persistence, and a bit of resignation to honestly look inside yourself to see what assumptions you hold that support your mental habits and why it is difficult for you to let them go. If you can't release the assumptions that hold together your paradigm of perfection, you will not complete your transformation. You will not be able to create a new sense of self because the old you with her promises of short-lived rewards will keep calling you back. To be free from the tyranny of the perfectionist paradigm, look for yourself in the following pages. Not everything will fit for you. If you accept what does fit, your transformation will begin today.

BEING PERFECT VERSUS BEING RIGHT

Here's the cycle: You start a job and quickly fall into the ranks of Perfectionist because you work hard to be right and amazing. You set and meet very high standards. You judge others against these standards even though they will never be able to clone you. You may respond with humility when people pay tribute to your intelligence, resourcefulness, and ability but you never tire of the accolades. You may be surprised, even appalled, when people call you a perfectionist, but your commitment to doing extraordinary work drains your happiness and strains your relationships on a par with the purist perfectionist. When it feels as though people have quit recognizing your contribution or the promotions and challenges have slowed down, you see no reason to stay. You begin to look for a different job with new, interesting projects and people who will be dazzled by your knowledge and work.

The three assumptions defined in the following pages keep you locked into this cycle because they feed your need of being the one who knows more and does everything best. These assumptions give you a sense of security even when the world is crashing around you. Essentially, they are your anchors. Yet, the more emotionally attached you are to these assumptions, the more the anchors lock in and keep you from growing. *The illusions you live by set you up for the inevitable disillusions you experience.* In the end, if you hold onto these assumptions, the path you wander will be an endless loop where you keep repeating the perfectionist cycle. The quicker you acknowledge and release these beliefs, the easier life will be.

Assumption 1

There is a right answer and it is mine (what, are you blind?).

If you are the best and the one who knows, then you have an answer for every question about things that are important to you, and no one dares to disagree. Others may have a similar answer but if they challenge your point of view, they are wrong. Even if you give their answers some credit, you will always find pieces to discount. Your actions, intentionally or not, demean others. If you are honest with yourself, you will admit that if you allow others to be right, your expertise will be questioned. You won't lose confidence in your knowledge and skills, but you do fear the loss of stature of being the most knowledgeable in the group.

The attachment to the assumption that you are always right keeps you on the defensive, especially if you are working with Queen, Warrior, or Rebel energies. Dissenters are outsiders who don't have a clue or, worse, they are traitors and enemies. From the moment they disagree with you, you quit trusting them and will hold them at arm's length in all your interactions. If you feel unappreciated or disrespected, you talk behind their back to get affirmation from others that you are right and they are wrong or ignorant. Think back to your last "woe is me" conversation with a friend. I bet your friend totally agreed with your negative valuation of your less-than-adoring colleagues. When your friends agree with your gossip, the social bond keeps you from feeling isolated when you push others away.[5]

Always being right not only hurts your relationships, but is also a heavy responsibility to bear. You have to work harder to discount other people's ideas than if you just looked for the value in their suggestions. Yet, because being the one who knows is foundational to your sense of self, you will feel uncomfortable letting go of this persona. It will take time for you to realize that life can be so much easier and healthier when you don't have to be right.

Opening my mind to the possibility that someone else could come up with a useful idea was a breakthrough in my relationship with my former boss. I was complaining to my coach about how my boss disrespected me by forcing me to accept his ideas without hearing mine when she explained that he was doing his best with the amount of light he had; his light was small while mine was large. I loved that explanation until she added, "Now, you have the responsibility to model what big light looks like." From that day forward, I slowed down my negative reactions to his contrary ideas. Funny thing—when I quieted my defensive mind enough to hear him out, I found some interesting kernels in what he proposed. When I began acknowledging his ideas, he in turn asked to hear mine, which he then praised. That's when I realized that two perfectionists will never have a satisfying discussion until one of them lowers the wall.

Another aspect of the assumption that you are right is that you may only take on jobs that you inherently know you can master. One of the real eye-openers that emerged from my interviews with the women for this book was the concept of "premeditated risk-taking." By nature, you appear to be a risk-taker. However, unless you carry the Gambler archetype, your risks are calculated and weighted toward probable success. Before you jump, you discern the dangers of the risk you are about to take. If there is a good shot at success, you'll go for it even if it means changing careers and trying something you have never done before. If you don't think you will be able to master the challenge, you'll pass. If you jump and it turns out to be deeper than you thought, you quickly look for a good excuse to move on. You won't dance if it makes you look stupid.

Unfortunately, your quick evaluation of a possible failure could keep you from expressing your imaginative and playful selves. While visiting Florida, I went out on a boat with friends. I was coaxed into steering the boat while it sped through the water. I followed directions and kept us on course, but I wasn't comfortable with the thought of maneuvering around other boats and wakes. As soon as I could, I passed the responsibility on to my boyfriend. Even after years of working to change my assumptions, when I am given a task where I know I will make mistakes in front of others, I back off. I travel the world by myself, I've changed jobs and industries numerous times, and I make major purchases without guidance, but I won't do anything that my brain surmises will lead to failure or even lead to a mediocre performance, which is a failure by my standards. Chances are, the same goes for you when you refuse to do anything that may look inept in the eyes of others. You won't see the lesson in it. Sadly, you won't see the pleasure in it, either. Risk-taking for you isn't really about risk; in the end you know you will perform well. There are no Clowns and childlike archetypes on your list although there should be. You won't know freedom until you are able to laugh at your silly self.

Assumption 2

Everything is up to me (this place is full of idiots).

This assumption implies that things will spin out of control or fail if you don't hold them together. Though individuals may work hard and have good ideas and skills to offer, no one has the overall perspective you have. You have no patience for ambiguity. You have little tolerance for innovation outside the lines drawn by your expectations. Ultimately, you will have to take charge of the project if it is going to be done right and on time.

As a result of this assumption, you will overwork, take on too many projects, and resist sharing your work with anyone else. Other women struggle with saying "no" so they don't disappoint someone else; you avoid the word for fear of disappointing yourself. You believe you can do it all and you love proving you can, so saying no betrays yourself. It is hard to say no when the project is new, visible, and a good avenue to utilize your talents. The problem is that you will then "own" the project and struggle with delegating authority and responsibilities. You like to do the work and you don't trust that others will perform as well as you.[6] You will also find it difficult being a part of a team and not being the leader. When you can't lead you have trouble feeling engaged unless the leader tactfully gives you a goal you can control on your own. Unless the team is made up of all "A" players, sharing responsibilities with your colleagues will be a stretch for you. You prefer to do your work while they do theirs.

At your lowest point when you are really unhappy, your stress becomes your badge of honor. You will complain about the idiots you work with and compete with your colleagues over who had the craziest day. When someone asks you how you are doing, you give the obligatory "fine" and add a sigh, a roll of the eyes, and a smile that ends with a frown. You deny yourself rare moments of peace with tasks from your to-do lists. You might even develop a pattern of being late to meetings because you have to read one more e-mail or check off one more task. Because everything is up to you and your work is extremely important, you have the right to be late.

Because you are an accomplished high achiever, the assumption that everything is up to you may be reinforced by your manager. Your colleagues and your team may also skirt the truth if you ask them directly for feedback. Don't assume you aren't too controlling, self-righteous, or condescending because no one has told you that you aren't. In order to break away from this assumption, you have to be aware of your actions and be honest with yourself when the impact is negative because you may not hear the truth from anyone else.

Assumption 3

I will always be disappointed (nothing or no one measures up).

I had hired a coach to help me figure out why I was having trouble maintaining long-term romantic relationships. I couldn't seem to find the right man. She asked me, "When will you give up your attachment to being disappointed by your relationships?" Her question took my breath away. She was right. Not long after I started a relationship, I began finding fault with my partner. Because each man was a normal, imperfect human, I always found what I was looking for. When the coach asked me the question about giving up my attachment to being disappointed, I came face-to-face with how my disappointment served me. The truth is, I expected to be disappointed before I ever gave the relationship a chance. Being disappointed with men released me from the hard work of sustaining a long-term relationship.

Being chronically disappointed with work is the same story as being chronically disappointed with your relationships. When you are attached to being disappointed with your job, your boss, or your company, you don't ever have to make a commitment to staying and working through problems. You will conveniently find reasons to leave. You will give everything you have to your job up front, demonstrating that you should be treasured. Then you will feel let down the moment you aren't recognized for your good work or you aren't given the best assignment. No matter how excited you were when you took the job, you knew it would be only a matter of time before the wind would blow and you, Wander Woman, would have to move on.

When you have an attachment to being disappointed, you never feel a complete sense of connection with your team, which makes it easier for you to write them off. You might have a few colleagues you bond with, but you quickly surmise who is worthy of being in your small tribe. According to Robert W. Fuller, most humans unconsciously separate people into the categories of Somebodies and Nobodies.[7] However, Fuller says most people use titles and status as their criteria for discrimination. Your criteria are different. Somebodies are your allies and people who admire you. Nobodies don't "get you" or your perspective. You might try to convince Nobodies to see the light. Eventually you write them off. When you accumulate enough Nobodies, you write off the company and start looking for your next opportunity.

To justify your behavior, you create standards that are difficult for anyone to meet. As soon as you feel a person or group is not on your side, you throw up your shield by using these standards to quickly find fault with what they are saying and doing. From this point on, they will rarely measure up. You treat them like people who don't know anything and either avoid them or brush them off by saying things like, "I don't have time for this" or "This makes no sense" or the definitive statement, ". . . because I said so." Whether you are speaking to clerks, assistants, colleagues, or your children, *you "nobody" people with both verbal and nonverbal weapons.* You aren't being intentionally cruel. You are just protecting your Queen, Commander, Thinker, or Scholar positions. I used to have an assistant who would hold up a mirror to me when I acted this way by saying, "Oh, you're in one of your moods." I hated and appreciated her courage.

If you don't release your attachment to disappointment, you will drift without a plan on a lonely boat. When you leave a company, you focus on what went wrong instead of what good things occurred that you can build on in your next job. If someone were to ask you to describe your last job, you easily detail what you resented about the frustrating corporate politics, the archaic rules and procedures, and the antics of your misinformed boss. Never mind that you met some great people and learned some important lessons. Disappointment leaves little room for good memories. If you had a plan and you left your job because the timing was right, would you better recognize what wisdom your experience gave you? Disappointment skews your view and steers you away from making long-term plans.

THERE IS MORE THAN ONE RIGHT ANSWER

When your mind is full of judgment it is using the mental resources you need to see opportunities. Therefore, the more strongly you hold on to these three assumptions, the more you will use your brain to find what is wrong about situations, leaving you less capable of finding opportunities for growth and pleasure. While you are busy being critical, you miss the help your boss tries to give you because it isn't what you want to hear. When you are pushing your point of view, you overlook an opportunity to align with a colleague. When you are busy being angry for not getting to work on the project you proposed, you do not see other doors opening for you.

Even if your judgment is justified in the moment, it doesn't serve you in the long run. It limits your choices. It reduces your power. You have to quiet your critical mind to see the world and yourself in a softer light. There are many answers to a complex problem. There are many ways to interpret a situation. There are many facets to each person you meet. Honestly, what is the purpose of staunchly protecting your opinions? You have now read many pages describing how harmful your judgment can be to your happiness and to the health of your relationships. Ask yourself what good your judgment does the next time your critical mind starts chattering.

The key to shifting out of always being right is *to consciously choose to learn* when you think you already know the answers. As a human, you cope with the complexity of life by having good reasons for what you think. Therefore, you are a master at rationalizing the particular behavior that has most helped you as a high achiever—your ability to be right. Because rationalizing is a survival instinct, the incidence of digging in and justifying your opinion kicks in instantly, much faster than the process for analyzing what is logical and possible. In order to override your lightning-fast rationalizations, you have to deliberately commit to accepting that there is more than one right way to achieve a goal and there is more than one right answer to a question. "There is always more than one" must become your mantra. If you say it enough times and remind yourself by leaving little notes around your office and home, you are not only opening your mind but expanding it with experiential knowledge.

One way to adjust your thinking is to first release the tension in your body, which gives you a chance to think before you speak. When your critical mind jumps in, your brain readies your body for a fight. Your muscles tense. Your heart starts pounding. You may even hold your breath and squint your eyes. If you can sense these physical reactions before you speak, you can better control your reactions. Release your breath before opening your mouth. This pausing technique gives you a moment to better assess the situation. Maybe the people you disagree with are right from their perspective, which differs from yours. Maybe they have a solution that will work as well as yours or better if you can admit it. Maybe your relationship is more important than the perfect result. So the true solution is to (1) see if you can use their ideas or (2) keep your mouth shut. When you release the tension in your body before you speak, you free your mind to see that you can respond in more than one way.

If you have the presence of mind, ask yourself if there is a truth you don't want to face that is prompting your irritation. When you are frustrated or disappointed by your boss or your peers, are you covering up a fear of losing your Superstar status? Could you be blaming others for your dissatisfaction with your job and your life? Are you restless because you're bored and you can't wait to find the next shiny thing to play with? You have to be brutally honest with yourself to choose what is really "right and good" for you in the end. You are a smart woman. You can call on your higher intelligence instead of your primitive, survivalist brain when assessing yourself and the situation you are facing.

TURN ON YOUR MENTAL MOVIE SET

In order to release yourself from your limiting beliefs, you need to first vision a successful life without them. Slowing down your critical mind is good practice for now. Visioning will help you crystallize the less critical, contented, purposeful self you want to create going forward. When you imagine what you want for yourself, your brain accepts these images as a test run that helps you start implanting new ideas before trying them out in real time. A study was done by Alvaro Pascual-Leone, a neurologist at Harvard, that found that when pianists listen to and envision themselves playing a piece of music, they activate the same areas in the brain as when they are actually moving their fingers.[8] The improvement of your interpersonal relationships can also be enhanced through the same kind of mental imaging. If you figure out what you want to do in specific situations and practice these actions and feelings in your head, your brain records your activity in your motor cortex where you have access to the memories even under duress. It's true that you can't account for all interpersonal situations, but you can prepare for upcoming interactions and presentations, which will help when you face unplanned events.

Be sure to include both *what you want to do* and *how you want to feel* when you vision to trigger the optimal neural connections. Your brain works most efficiently when you are feeling happy, grateful, proud, compassionate, hopeful, forgiving, receptive, lucky, confident, optimistic, or any emotions related to feeling good.[9]

The more you repeat your visioning exercises, the more you ingrain the map you want your brain to follow. The map could define an event in the future or it could detail tomorrow's staff meeting. If you are creating tomorrow's meeting, include who you want to be and how you want to feel from the time you walk through the door. What archetypes will express themselves during the meeting? Imagine yourself comfortably saying "no" to a project or asking for help instead of doing it all yourself. After the meeting, see yourself taking a break without guilt to reflect on how the meeting went. Then plan to join your favorite colleagues for lunch and take a brisk walk around the building to re-energize before reimmersing yourself in your work. If you want to drop your armor and become a wonderfully imperfect, accepting, and gracious human who listens as well as she speaks, vision yourself modeling these behaviors and emotions every day until the images becomes your reality.

Create this mental movie in a spot where you feel comfortable and where you can either dream or write your narrative with no interruptions. Ideally, you will make this a nightly ritual before you go to bed. This allows your brain to process the images while you sleep. What would tomorrow look like if, at the end of the day, you feel as energized as when you started? Include what it will take to be more content with your work and happy with the people you work with. Include all your senses when visualizing. Touch, hear, smell, and taste the things you see as you move through your day. Your visions should be sensual as well as visual so your brain will record the events as if you are actually experiencing them.

Define your vision in concrete visual terms loaded with nouns and verbs. Adjectives, such as the word *good* in "I will be a good parent" or the word *successful* in "I will be a successful manager" are too vague to use as a guide. See the specific actions you are taking, step by step, as you are being a good parent or successful leader. Be sure to see each experience you are visioning from the beginning to the end. Most people just see themselves starting an event. A good start doesn't ensure a happy ending. See yourself complete the experience, including how good you feel when you walk out the door.

Your vision should go beyond the reality of today while staying in the realm of possibility. Visions should help you stretch beyond your comfort zone. Allow yourself to create the possibility before you kill it with doubt and pessimism. However, don't include fantasies that would truly take divine intervention to attain. For example, don't add inches to your height and don't vision yourself becoming CEO tomorrow when you aren't even close. Visioning and hallucinating are two entirely different practices.

• •

EXERCISE: Your Ten-Minute Daily Visioning Session

Take ten minutes before you go to sleep or while you lie in bed in the morning to quietly view your new day in your mind. See yourself get out of bed and then watch your day go by as if it were a movie with a happy ending. Include specific events you have scheduled or would like to happen. Remember to focus on who you are being and how you are feeling throughout your day. How would you like your relationships to play out? What does your communication look like and what is its impact? What do you need to do to be effective as a leader? Which archetypes will be most useful to you? How often do you laugh? Do you take time to thank others for their efforts? Include moments where you notice what you are grateful for and what delights you during your imperfect, wonderful day.

Do this exercise consistently for twenty-one days. It takes twenty-one days of focus to form a new neural network, meaning your visions will become your default thinking. To actually change your behavior, continue your visioning practice for three months. If you make it a ritual, visioning should become a habit. Extend the habit to 180 days and you will be a new person at work.

When you complete your vision, ask yourself, "Am I willing to do what it takes to make my vision real?" The answer to this question indicates your willingness to begin the process of transformation. You must commit to consistent rituals to create new default behavior.

• • • •

You can also call on your Board of Directors archetypes for help in creating new visions. Assemble your archetypes. Review a situation you are struggling with. Declare your interpretation of why people are behaving a certain way and why you are responding as you are. Then ask each of your archetypes in your circle how they would interpret and respond to the situation differently. What would your Inspirer do? Your Revolutionary? Your Connector? Your Artist? When you look at your dilemma through the different energies, you are likely to see options that you were blind to before. Weigh the advice the archetypes give you. Weave these ideas into your vision for a few nights and see what happens during the day. As things begin to change, you can go back to your Board for a new perspective. How you create success based on connection and creativity instead of on your personal accomplishments is going to be an ongoing conversation.

In addition to creating your vision, it is just as critical to find a moment at the end of your workday to review how well your day matched up with your vision. In addition to recognizing when you didn't behave as you would have liked, Marion Woodman, author of *Addiction to Perfection*, suggests asking yourself questions such as, "When did I laugh today? What made me feel pleasure?"[10] Identify the best of your days so you can increase the good in your next visioning session. You will be given directions in the next chapter on how to use this type of reflection not only to self-correct but also to uncover what new beliefs and behaviors will bring you even greater joy.

THE KEYWORD TO HAPPINESS

If you vision ten minutes a day in total belief that what you see will occur, you can then access pertinent elements of your vision throughout the day with a single "keyword." You don't need to repeat your entire vision again during the day. In fact, it is better to vision once a day and put it aside until the next night or morning. When you try to bring your vision into focus during the day, you tend to revert to criticizing yourself and noticing how the present doesn't live up to your vision. Even worse, when you are under pressure, trying to recall your entire vision will add to your frustration. Instead, if you catch yourself being right, bossy or elitist, you can stop the action and put yourself back on course with a single word. This word acts as the reset button without you having to assume the lotus position and replay your vision. It will help you stay on course until the next evening or morning when you engage in your ten-minute brain retraining session.

I learned about the power of using keywords from a professional golfer. In pressure-packed moments where he had to perform well, he found that thinking of one well-chosen word, which he called "a swing thought," would bring his brain back into focus and alleviate his fear of choking. You can use your keyword to keep from choking when your boss ticks you off, your team seems clueless, and all you want to do is knock some sense into the people around you. Using one word to activate your recall gives your brain the cue to put elements of your vision into play.

Like the golf pro, you want to choose one "swing thought" to redirect your thoughts back to what you determined you wanted to do and feel in the moment. Did your vision focus on you being patient, persuasive, compassionate, innovative, or inspiring? Choose one of these words to be your keyword. Are you focused on bringing in the energy of a particular archetype? Choose the title of your archetype to be the word that restores your sanity. You may use the word "future" to help you remember that this moment is simply another lesson that will help you meet your future goals. You might use the keyword "blessing" if you are trying to be more grateful for what the present is giving you, such as the gifts of experience, money for starting your own business, or time to be with your children.

When I started public speaking, I would put a Post-it® note somewhere in my view with three big letters spelling "fun." I knew that if I had fun on the stage, so would my audience. Each time I looked at the note, I quit worrying about giving a perfect performance. As soon as I calmed down and felt more playful, I gave the presentation I had envisioned with authenticity and fun. Now I use the keyword "care" when I speak to remind myself of my purpose for being on the platform. When I remember to care, my connection is more profound.

• •

✎ **EXERCISE**: Choosing Your Keyword

After you end a visioning session, declare one word that sums up your vision. Say it out loud. Write it down. Put it in your car, tape it to your cell phone or laptop, make it your screensaver or set it to show up as an appointment on your calendar. When your day starts to spin out of control, take a breath, center yourself in the moment, and fill your head with only your keyword. The keyword unlocks the mental door to the acceptance, patience, focus, and trust you need to live out your vision.

• • • •

YOU CAN'T GET AN A IN PERSONAL GROWTH

Committing to growth is itself a lesson in humility, patience, and imperfection. You can't be perfect when it comes to transformation. The exercises take more time than you want to give. The process is slow and will tax your patience. The good news is that the more quickly you admit to your assumptions, begin your visioning practice, and start using your keywords, the more quickly the new you will emerge.

There are still a few more things you need to do to master your thinking. Self-awareness and visioning create new connections in your brain while weakening other connections. Yet the weaker ones are still there. Deciding you don't want a habit, assumption, or self-concept anymore doesn't mean it will peacefully go away. You still need to work to limit the reruns. In the next chapter you will learn dialogue and presencing techniques so that when the old thoughts reappear, they will seem so out-of-place you can easily spot them and release them from your awareness. Commit to practicing these processes and you will take control of your thoughts.

FIVE

Opening the Windows

Karl and I were rushing to gas up a rental car before returning it to the airport. We forgot to calculate the trip to the gas station into the time needed to catch our flight. Luckily, we found a station on the way. His job was to fill the tank, mine was to pay. I pressed the appropriate keys under the screen at the pump and inserted my credit card. Nothing happened. I tried again. Nothing happened. I acted as I typically do when handling uncooperative electronics—I jammed my card into the slot multiple times while cursing at it. Before I could determine my next step, Karl leaped to my side and began giving me instructions on how to insert the card correctly. Because I am a smart and resourceful woman, my brain reacted by thinking, "Do you think I'm an idiot?" while my mouth said, "I know what to do!" I backed him off with glaring eyes and marched into the office. The clerk behind the counter was trying to quiet a line of complaining customers. The computer wasn't recognizing anyone's credit cards. It also wasn't recognizing cash, so we had to move on. Fortunately, the clerk shouted the location of another station about a mile away.

As we drove to the other station, I took a deep breath and said to Karl, "I'm sorry for biting your head off. I tend to react when someone tells me what to do unless I ask for their help. I know you meant well. I am working on not being so reactive. I'm getting better but I'm not sure I'm going to completely stop reacting in this lifetime."

He smiled and said, "Thank you. I understand. I tend to

react when someone looks stressed and in need. I jump in to help, maybe too soon. I'll work on it but I'm not sure I'm going to completely stop in this lifetime." My body melted into laughter. He squeezed my hand and said, "Anything else?"

His words opened the door for an easy conversation about how strong our relationship is because we talk about difficult situations soon after they happen. Incidents like this one remind me of how much I appreciate having Karl as my partner. He knows and loves the many faces of Marcia, including the new ones I'm working to embrace. More important, he helps me to laugh at myself. We are learning how to navigate this journey called life together. I once heard that you know your relationship is working because you are working on it. This description certainly characterizes my relationship with Karl. Whenever there are rough spots, we talk about them immediately, knowing that whatever we figure out will help us grow together. Our relationship is a developmental process that takes time, hopefully a lifetime.

When we talked in the car, we were using our "window of opportunity" to make a lasting change. If we had waited until we had a quiet moment together to talk, we might have skipped the conversation. Over time, the conflict-avoiding mechanism in the brain tends to trivialize the need to talk, fueling the rationalization that the issue is no longer important enough to discuss. Even if one of us had brought up the issue hours or days later, we would likely have ended up arguing over some detail that we remembered differently instead of discussing what we needed to resolve. We would have lost the best opportunity to learn from the situation if we had put off the conversation for a more convenient time. Talking shortly after the interaction occurred gave us both the chance to explain, explore, acknowledge, apologize, and even laugh at our behavior. From here, we could determine how to better honor each other's needs and idiosyncrasies in the future.

A window of opportunity exists after any mind-rattling event where you can step out of your frame and evolve, but the time you have to access this window is limited. Whether you just learned something in a classroom, suffered an embarrassing incident, or engaged in a heated conversation over dinner, if you wait too long to talk about and act on what you discovered, the window closes. Short-term memory has limited capacity. In fact, only a few ideas you read in this book will stick regardless of how many notes you write in the margins.[1] You might increase your retention rate if you tell someone what you liked about the chapter, yet you are still using your temporary short-term memory if you don't take what you read deeper into your brain through reflection, dialogue, and repeated actions.[2] This fact is especially true for women, who tend to learn better than men through verbal processing.[3] If you don't take advantage of your window of opportunity after you read or experience something new, your brain will quickly rationalize itself back to status quo.

Unfortunately, we spend more time ingesting information than we do gaining long-lasting wisdom from what we read, listen to, and experience. Most of the women I interviewed claimed learning to be one of their highest values. Many accumulate degrees as if it were their hobby. If not degrees, they consume books, teleseminars, podcasts, and videos during their free time to fill in the gaps. The never-ending quest to be "in-the-know" on subjects is addictive. They have to consume facts, gossip, and predictions to stay ahead. Yet how much of this information do they actually retain? Like these women, you may store megabits of data that you can regurgitate at a meeting or cocktail party. However, if all you do is consume the information and move on, it's unlikely that any of the facts will change your self-concept and behavior. If you do not take the time to write and dialogue about what you are learning, the window of opportunity for growing closes.[4] What you watch, read, or listen to becomes noise passing through your head.

This chapter will teach you how to embed wisdom into your brain using reflection, Appreciative Dialogue, and presencing techniques. Think back to the last time you had a blinding flash of insight . . . can you remember what it was? If you didn't talk about the insight or find a way to apply the learning, your grand thought disappeared. You have to lock the learning into your brain so that when the challenges of life appear, you can retrieve your insights, which then lead to new possibilities to try. The exercises in this chapter will help you learn and retain the bits of information you need to flex your thoughts and behavior when you want to.

In addition to decreasing the natural atrophy of learning, taking advantage of your window of opportunity will give you new fodder for your visioning ritual. Because you love new challenges and prefer to vary your activities, you are apt to get bored with the visioning exercise if you don't keep refreshing the pages. Ideas for change may come to you during the day as you notice the effects of your behavior. Jotting down a note to yourself on a scrap of paper or recording your ideas on your telephone do little to change your mind. However, you can use the memo later to start a discussion. The best way to turn your thoughts into permanent new pathways in your brain is to engage in a focused, Appreciative Dialogue soon after the event occurs.

APPRECIATIVE DIALOGUE: THE GIFT OF GAB

As I mentioned in chapter 3, your notion of self is defined in the patterns of interconnectivity between neurons in the brain. You are what you feel and what you think about throughout the day. These neural patterns in your brain are not static; they are shifting all the time. Yet the brain will stretch and then return to the same patterns if you aren't intentional about your learning. Behavioral change thus takes a very long time if you leave your brain to its own devices.[5] I have given you some ways of increasing the speed of change through working with archetypes and daily visioning. Yet your work up until now has taken place in your own head when you find a moment to be silent. You can accelerate the process of shifting your self-concept by taking the time to verbally explore the meaning and possibilities of what is taking place throughout the day. When you talk about what you learned after experiencing a difficult interaction or reading an interesting passage, you are using verbal exploration and discovery to fire up neurons and create new connections in your brain.

Therefore, if you are looking to expand your self-concept, not only do you want to have new experiences, but you also need to find people you trust and respect to talk with about the positive aspects of your experiences. You need to evaluate, discuss, reveal, uncover, connect, and mentally leap forward in the presence of someone else. Your dialogue partner should be someone who will not judge you when you speak and who believes in your highest potential. If you aren't working with a coach, find at least two friends who are on similar journeys whom you can dialogue with. You need at least two friends just in case one is not available when you want to talk. If you can develop an entire support group of women committed to helping each other grow both their careers and their happiness, you can definitely speed up the re-creation process. I will share ideas on how to form a network in chapter 7, including more specific criteria to help you choose the right partners for you. Keep in mind that because you and your friends are often too busy to maintain regular conversations, hiring a professional coach to facilitate your reflection is a perfect complement to your cache of colleagues.

When you engage your friends or a coach in an *Appreciative Dialogue*, you place a microscope on specific situations so you can find what is good to carry forward. Appreciative Dialogue is based on the popular approach to organizational change called Appreciative Inquiry designed by David L. Cooperrider and his associates at Case Western Reserve University in the mid-1980s. The approach has proven to improve performance by engaging people in discussing and building on what's working rather than trying to fix what's not.[6] When you have an Appreciative Dialogue with your friend or coach, you first define your values, your hopes, and your passion. Then you explore what is helping you to move forward so you can leave behind what is not. You analyze what assumptions drove you to make certain decisions and then brainstorm what other beliefs could work for you. You can laugh at some of the crazy things you do to gain recognition, control, and attention, which can help you discover what might give you better results in the future. You dream out loud about what is possible for you and what you can truly do to make a difference when you stand in the power and the grace of your gifts.

Because you probably can't talk about your experiences with someone every day, you can still keep your windows of opportunity open between live conversations by writing your reflections in a journal. The act of sitting and writing about your observations, thoughts, and feelings provides focus and clarity to your issues and concerns.[7] Reflective writing can lead you to recognize your habitual thought patterns. The free flow of expression makes it easier for you to explore your thoughts more deeply than when you just roll them around in your brain. Writing helps you peel back layers of rationalizations to discover the beliefs and desires that weren't readily apparent to you before. When you come face-to-face with the destructive nature of these patterns you naturally open doors to possible alternatives.

Remember that the focus is appreciative even when you journal. Don't dwell too long on what went wrong. Instead discover what strengths and feelings you can call upon to improve these situations and then imagine the myriad of options you can try. The next step is to try out these possibilities or discuss them further with your dialogue partner or coach. Combining reflective writing with Appreciative Dialogue gives you a tangible experience of your mental evolution.

THE MAGIC OF AN APPRECIATIVE FOCUS

I was coaching a woman who was struggling with her decision to partner with a colleague on a new business venture. Her resistance had nothing to do with the dangers in the new partnership. They both had clients waiting to hire them. She was excited about the leadership program they had designed and she loved working with her colleague. To secure their relationship, they drew up a contract with a lawyer to define the partnership going forward and the terms if they split up. Everything seemed perfect except for the nagging notion that kept her up at night telling her she was making a mistake. Every time she tried to box up the program she had been delivering for the past two years, she couldn't do it. The program had been her lifeline. When she left her corporate job, she landed a few contracts that kept her above water financially until she was asked to teach a sales training course. She came up with a unique process she taught to managers in a variety of large retail companies to help them lead their teams to success. The program took off and secured her status as a successful entrepreneur. She still had many requests for the program. Yet she had grown tired of delivering it. She had never taken the time to develop the materials to replicate the program as a licensed or salable product and she didn't have the energy to do this work now. Yet how could she justify sticking it on a shelf? She felt terribly guilty and was concerned that she was making a poor decision based on boredom instead of good sense.

I asked her to describe to me what pieces of the sales

program she had carried forward into her new venture. She easily detailed six elements, including the structure of the follow-up segments. I asked her to list five things she contributed to the success of the sales program that would help her be successful with the new venture. First, she named the enthusiasm she had when she delivered the course the first two years. She knew she would deliver the new program with even more enthusiasm. She was very excited about both the program itself and the possible impact she and her colleague could have on leaders around the world, which clearly tied into her sense of purpose. Then she listed four things she contributed that helped people retain the information, including having the participants (1) engage in peer coaching, (2) integrate what they were learning into their daily goals, (3) align their goals to personal visions, and (4) celebrate their efforts no matter what were the results. She said she had adapted these four elements to her own life as well. She then said she had incorporated three of these elements into the new program and would find a way to blend in the fourth one. I asked her, "Have you really killed off your first program?" She laughed and admitted that the sales program was alive and well in everything she did today. She wasn't leaving anything behind. She was just taking another step in her journey. Besides, the program would always be there if she decided to offer it again in the future. Her guilt vanished with her discovery that she was simply moving forward, not leaving anything behind. She felt content that her wandering was a strategy instead of a silly impulse.

Whereas visioning sets the context for the future, Appreciative Dialogue helps you explore the present moment and events in a way very different from typical problem solving. You aren't just analyzing options and making decisions. You are asked to view situations differently to see if there is a perspective you missed that could help you move forward. In fact, the sorting and arranging of information involved in typical problem-solving processes works against your ability to see the problem in a new light. You can try to shift and rearrange what you know, but your thoughts end up swirling around in circles in your short-term memory. Wracking your brain for solutions can be very frustrating. Many times you will give up and keep doing what you have always done or try something new simply because it is different from what you have tried before. *The sudden, new, and amazing solution to a problem only arises when you can look at your situation from an entirely new angle.* Taking an appreciative approach to problems, you are asked to see through a lens of positivity, not the normal critical lens where you negatively judge yourself and others.[8]

It is very difficult to shift your brain out of typical problem-solving processes to manifest an insightful discovery on your own. Because the brain likes to quickly assign meaning and solutions to what you see, disarming these constructs is hard to do by yourself unless you are an Artist by nature. You increase the possibility of seeing things differently when you work with someone who will ask you questions that make you think outside of the box that your logical brain likes to play in. Coaches who specialize in helping you see beyond the obvious solutions will ask questions that associate concepts you would not have linked on your own. The questions they ask create a new awareness that seems to "pop" into your brain. The discovery generally happens in an instant, or what is called an "Aha" moment. You not only see things differently, but the "Aha" always triggers a strong emotion that sparks activity in the middle brain and long-term memory, which helps you remember the breakthrough forever.

Whether you are exploring with a coach or a friend, when you engage in deeply appreciative conversations with someone you trust, life becomes a fascinating learning experience. When someone else listens, values your journey wherever you are, and is sincerely curious enough to ask you thoughtful, nonjudgmental questions, your brain senses no threat, which frees you to explore deeper meanings and possibilities. What you believe to be true literally changes. You realize there is more than one reality for any situation. When you see what else could be true related to your experience, new solutions naturally follow. You can never go back to being stuck in your old ways of thinking.

Using Appreciative Dialogue to sort out personal challenges goes beyond discovering and applying your strengths. As a high achiever, you can easily identify what you are good at doing. Yet being smart and capable doesn't necessarily give you the joy of feeling excited and alive. Appreciative Dialogue goes beyond assessing your strengths to being mindful of the moments where you feel fully alive and excited about your future. You explore everything that you personally contributed to the creation of your peak experiences in the past and then consciously apply those contributions—your strengths, archetypes, values, and outside resources—to a challenge you are currently facing.

HOW TO HAVE AN APPRECIATIVE DIALOGUE

Appreciative Dialogue can be used after both positive and negative experiences where you were stirred to feel. You then capitalize on your window of opportunity after the event by having a focused dialogue with someone who is able to keep the conversation on an appreciative track.

Let's first look at using Appreciative Dialogue to help deal with a negative experience or problem. If you had a dark-side reaction such as annoyance, rage, betrayal, disgust, fear, or embarrassment, as soon as you could you would stop and explore peak experiences in your past when you felt energized, significant, and fulfilled. List what you did to create your peak experiences. Looking at your list, you then seek how to apply what you discovered to your difficult situation. How can you look at the present moment in light of your peak experiences? What is available to you to shift from dark to light? New ideas will appear in the conversation as you connect your positive past with the present moment. The intent of Appreciative Dialogue is to teach your brain how to make the shift from problems to possibilities.

I used Appreciative Dialogue with a client to help her find the perfect job. She had left her job late in 2008 in the middle of the global economic crisis because she couldn't tolerate the way the leaders in her company were trying to scare everyone into performing better. When most people were hunkering down in jobs they did not like because they were afraid they couldn't find another job, my client was a true Wander Woman and chose to leave. Because she was highly educated with twenty years of experience in her field, she felt she could easily get another job. After three months of hitting dead ends, she called me in a panic. She had been visioning her new job every day. She was networking as best she could and was working with a few powerful headhunters. Yet more doors were closing than opening. She wondered if she should lower her expectations and take a lesser job.

I asked her to think back to the time she was most alive, engaged, and fulfilled by her work. She described a time when she helped to implement a major organizational change where she ignited passion in the employees who could see the vision while she maintained the dignity of those who were asked to leave. I then asked her to look more deeply at her personal contribution to this experience. What did she bring to the table to make this transition work so well? She said she not only designed an innovative solution, but she also formulated a unique plan to inspire the employees to participate. She facilitated groups where she listened and then used coaching skills to shift employees into taking positive action. She enlisted a few top executives to champion her programs. Although it was hard at times, she courageously held to her plan. In short, she was innovative, inspirational, committed, patient, a good coach, and a courageous leader who knew how to ask for help. I asked her how important these attributes would be to a company she wanted to work for today. She answered that her abilities were critical for helping companies emerge strongly from the economic crisis.

I started to ask her if she had included these attributes in her résumé when she interrupted me with her insight. "I can't believe I've just been sitting back waiting for other people to find me a job. I'm not a normal job candidate. I should be calling key people and telling them what I can do for their companies. I'm a Magician. They need me." She then talked nonstop about her plan for pinpointing the companies she wanted to work for and how she would find the right people inside the companies to talk to. She also formulated a new pitch for her headhunters. Instead of feeling hopeless, she left the call feeling energized, significant, and positive about her next job. She e-mailed me later that day to tell me how excited one of the headhunters was after they spoke because he now had a clearer picture of the power of the person he was trying to sell.

Appreciative Dialogue brings the best of the past into the present moment. As a result, my client wasn't asked to fill a position in any company. Instead, she was asked to recreate her best work for a growing company that hired her first as a consultant and then created a full-time position just for her.

When you use Appreciative Dialogue, you explore a challenge by applying your best self so your brain can recall pictures of success instead of what you want to avoid. In his studies about how the brain processes information, Cooperrider found that the brain doesn't respond to the word "not." If someone tells you, "don't think about elephants," your brain responds by digging up a picture of an elephant from your memory and placing it front and center in your mind.[9] This works even without words. Have you ever been riding a bicycle when you noticed a rock in the road? No matter what you do to avoid hitting the rock, you hit the rock. If instead you focus on what a good day it is to ride, you more easily maneuver around the obstacle. You are applying the same principle when you discuss how to apply your best self to a situation to get positive results instead of focusing all your energy on trying to fix what went wrong. I could have asked my client what she thought wasn't working in her approach to find a new job and she might have discovered a few things she could do better in the approach she had been taking. I doubt the conversation would have been as rich and inspirational compared to the Appreciative Dialogue we had that moved her into a concerted, positive effort to find a great new job.

• •

EXERCISE: Using Appreciative Dialogue for Problem Solving

When faced with a difficult situation or shortly after an unsettling conflict, explore the following questions with a coach or trusted friend:

1. Describe a peak experience where you felt fully alive and fulfilled.
2. What five things did you contribute to creating this peak experience?
3. What can you carry forward to the challenge you are now facing or what will help you to better understand the difficult situation you just experienced?
4. What is possible for you now?

• • • •

You can also use Appreciative Dialogue to extend and repeat a positive experience where you feel pride, appreciation, elation, amusement, and a sense of peace. The focus is on "what can I continue?" instead of on "what's next?"

You then detail what you did to create the glorious moment so you know specifically what you will repeat. Contemplating positive experiences provides a balance for the time you spend focusing on the difficult situations you face. No matter how many good things happen in a day, you often go home complaining about what your boss didn't do or how your colleagues fumbled. When you use Appreciative Dialogue to explore what went right in your day, you not only lighten up your mood, you also give your central nervous system a much-needed rest.

• •

EXERCISE: Using Appreciative Dialogue to Expand Possibilities

After experiencing a fulfilling and enjoyable experience, explore the following questions with a coach or trusted friend:

1. What five things did I specifically do to feel so alive and fulfilled?
2. What can I carry forward to ensure this experience happens more often?
3. What else is possible for me?

• • • •

You should have a few people in your support network who are skilled in Appreciative Dialogue to take advantage of your windows of opportunity before they close. If you are working through this book with other women in your network, the following guidelines will help you set the stage for your conversations. Remember to have these conversations often so you can determine what activities, mindset, and archetypes will best serve you right now. The results will help you adjust and revitalize your daily vision.

Appreciative Dialogue: Rules for the Road

1. *Your partner asks questions and rephrases/summarizes your answers.* Your dialogue partner will not offer you suggestions. She will ask questions to help you clarify what *abilities*, *mindsets*, and *actions* you can carry forward on your journey to create more peak experiences. She may also hold a mirror up by reflecting, rephrasing, and summarizing what you are saying. If she says something you don't agree with, accept the thoughts as interesting viewpoints and determine whether there is a common ground to build on. If your partner persists in offering a suggestion or her opinion, ask her to honor the rules of Appreciative Dialogue. You can then decide if the conversation feels productive and should be continued or suspended.
2. *Say "yes" to the reflections and questions your partner offers.* As long as your partner is not offering a suggestion or opinion, if you find yourself resisting the line of inquiry, stop and explore your resistance. Remember that Appreciative Dialogue is not a linear conversation in search of solutions. It is a vertical, deep exploration with the intention to better understand what living as your best self looks and feels like.
3. *Take time to think.* Truth emerges in dialogue. If you feel you need personal time to ponder a truth that is revealed, you can end the session by stating your intention to spend time thinking about what has transpired. Be sure to write down the truth you discovered because insights are transient if they do not lead to immediate action.
4. *Do not ignore your emotions.* Talk about what you are

feeling and what you think prompted your reactions. Exploring the possible reasons for any emotion that shows up is a significant part of the process.

5. *Do not argue with or criticize yourself.* Your partner has permission to stop you from falling into a negative analysis and to ask you to return to an appreciative perspective.

6. *Don't expect immediate results.* You are in a "discovery zone" where you are seeking to define your future based on what brings you joy instead of analyzing what you need to correct. There may be no measurable output at the end of your dialogue. Learning may be immediate or could be revealed over time.

FOUR STEPS TO CENTER YOUR AWARENESS IN THE PRESENT MOMENT

You may vision possibilities before you face an experience and then take advantage of your window of opportunity after the experience is over, yet the choice to actually change your emotions and behavior is made in the present. Therefore, you have to be an observer as well as a participant in the moment so you know when it's a perfect time to shift. It doesn't serve you to have a keyword if you aren't aware of when you need to summon your vision. For example, in order to shift from irritation to calm or from anger to determination, you need to be conscious of when you first slip into feeling irritated or angry. This is the moment you will want to engage your vision or call forth a different archetype.

Yet immediate awareness doesn't seem to be the natural state of the adult mind. Your brain is so saturated by the deluge of cell phones, computers, constant noise, crowds to avoid, and the steady stream of inner chatter that you forget to stop and notice what is going on inside you. Or, worse, you say you don't have time to pay attention. In his classic book *Self-Renewal*, John Gardner wrote, "Human beings have always employed an enormous amount of clever devices for running away from themselves. We keep ourselves so busy, fill our lives with so many diversions, stuff our heads with so much knowledge, involve ourselves with so many people and cover so much ground that we never have time to probe the fearful and wonderful world within. By middle life, most of us are accomplished fugitives from ourselves."[10] When life around you is doing its best to steal your attention, you have to consciously claim time to pay attention to yourself.

The more complex your life is, the harder it will be for you to stay present and notice what you are doing and feeling. You may even find it difficult to recall a peak experience because you don't recognize when you are feeling happy. You have to stop thinking about how many e-mails you have to read, what you want to buy for dinner, when you need to leave to avoid the traffic, why your boss didn't smile at you in the hallway, or who you need to invite to your next meeting. No matter how hard you try, worries and unfinished work creep into the crevices of your brains, pulling you away from what is going on right now. You can zone out practically anywhere and still survive, even while you drive. Add the myriad of tasks you are trying to accomplish at once to the steady stream of thoughts in your head and you become, as Gardner said, estranged from yourself. No wonder you feel lost if you take the time to think about where your life is going.

Staying present to the moment means keeping your mind fully focused on the world right in front of you and how you are interacting with it, which includes what you are feeling. Most professional athletes are trained on how to focus in the present as they warm up for a competition. Instead of zoning out, they zone in. Many actors received similar training. Earlier in my career, I created a set of audio programs that taught how to "be in the zone" based on ideas gleaned from interviews with athletes, sports psychologists, and acting coaches. I developed the following technique for the audiotapes and have since taught these steps to people around the world in programs on leadership, emotional intelligence, and coaching. Practicing these four steps will help you pay attention to what is happening inside your body and mind in the present moment.[11]

The Four Steps

1. *Relax* your body.
2. *Detach* from the thoughts running in your head.
3. Bring the *Center* of your body into your awareness.
4. *Focus* on how you want to feel and who you want to be.

1. Relax

When you experience stress, your brain initiates a physical response before logic is engaged. You hold or shorten your breath, your muscles tense up and blood is directed away from the brain to your large muscle groups. You must first release the tension in your body in order to take back control of your brain.

The fastest way to regulate your body is to focus on your breath. When stressed, you either stop or shorten your breathing. A delicious drink of oxygen will counteract stress and return your body to a state of harmony. Take in and release one deep breath.

Now focus on creating an easy breathing rhythm. Next, release the tension in your neck, back, arms, and legs to stimulate blood flow. Start by relaxing the muscles in your forehead and jaw. Then move your attention down your body. Loosen your neck muscles, drop your shoulders toward the ground, shake out your arms and legs, and uncurl your toes. You can also tighten and release your muscles a few times to encourage your muscles to relax. Do this mental scan and muscle release two or three times throughout your busy, task-filled day. You will find you have more energy to enjoy your evening once you finally quit working.

When you engage in activities that relax your body on a regular basis, you will live with less tension even during your adrenaline-packed days. In addition to doing routine body scans, exercise and stretch your muscles at least a few times a week to keep them loosened up. Try yoga, qigong, and other mind-calming physical practices to balance your heavy mental schedule. If you want to try something drastically different than what is customary, deliberately slow down your everyday tasks. Eat more consciously, drive more slowly, and walk at a gentle pace. As a high achiever, you are probably laughing at this suggestion. In reality, slowing down adds only a few minutes to what you are doing. These few minutes can make a huge difference in your happiness level. If you keep your body relaxed, you'll make better decisions and have far more capacity to deal with frustrations. Living life will feel much easier.

2. *Detach*

After you relax your body, then it's time to free up your mind by detaching from the judgmental chatter in your brain. Cleaning out the clutter makes space for possibilities. What thoughts carry the most weight in your brain? Among the heaviest thoughts are the judgments you form when talking to someone. As soon as you begin to negatively judge someone who doesn't live up to your high standards, you hear less of what they are saying. I find that if I just take in and release my breath and clear my mind, the person who is annoying me isn't that difficult after all. Of equal weight to your judgments are your concerns about how other people may judge you. Most high achievers want their brilliance recognized. Acting coach Gary Austin insists, "It's none of your business what people think of you." He says your business is to give 100 percent to what you are trying to accomplish. "For every moment you give to thinking about how someone is judging you, you are detracting from your best performance."[12] Unless the people you are talking to are falling asleep or rolling their eyes, quit worrying about what people are thinking and you will perform so well that their opinions of you won't matter. You can always ask for positive suggestions when you are done.

The paradox is that to control your mind you have to empty it. You can see this rule applied when you participate in something just for the fun of it. When you have nothing to lose, you are most likely to do your best. You sink your longest putt, deliver a top-notch speech, and find the win-win solution. When you erase thoughts about the past and the future, you're free to plunge into the present.

Practice detaching by consciously stopping your thoughts for thirty seconds while observing the world around you. Tomorrow, increase your practice to one minute. Each day, see how much longer you can notice your world around you without thinking. Then practice this detaching exercise the next time you are upset. You will give your brain a better chance to determine if your judgments and worries are worth the effort.

Four Tips for Detaching

1. Focus on what you can control.

When you focus on what you can't control, such as the work styles of others, unreasonable organizational policies, and the way things used to be, your brain fixates on what it can't have. The more you focus on your losses, the more difficult it will be to clear your mind. To help yourself detach, shift your focus to what you can control, such as taking care of yourself, working on goals that excite you, and planning your next adventure. It's easier to control your thoughts when you direct your brain to focus on what is in your control.

2. Let go of what you thought would happen.

You naturally have an expectation of how a situation will turn out. Then something else happens. If you aren't flexible, you will feel frustrated and annoyed. Ask yourself, "What is true about my situation now?" If you choose to work with what is happening now, whether you like it or not, you will probably find a way to make it work for you. Remember, there are many times in life when you don't get what you want, yet the results turn out to be better than you had expected. Have faith in your resourcefulness. Luck is having the presence of mind to see an opportunity when it arises.

3. Laugh at yourself.

Taking your work seriously is admirable. Taking yourself too seriously is not. Your sense of humor is your reality check on what should be seen as serious and what could be deemed as the silliness of human nature. Laugh at yourself first and then share the perspective with others. Your sense of fun will decrease stress and increase productivity.

4. Don't give up.

If you can't detach today, you may next time . . . or the next time after that. You are teaching your old brain a new trick. When you get frustrated, annoyed, irritated, or disappointed and forget to take a breath, forgive yourself before your brain gives you the perfect rationalization for your reaction. Then take an appreciative perspective to see what strengths, archetypes, values, and outside resources you can apply the next time you face a similar situation.

3. Center

According to many traditions, the true center of the mind lies in the center of the body. "Trust your gut." "Listen to the voice deep inside you." "Ask your body what you should do." These statements are some of the many aphorisms that point to a well of wisdom beyond the physical boundaries of your brain. To access this well, you have to move your awareness out of your head and into the core of your body—an act known as centering. Some people say your core is the central point just below the navel. Martial artists call this spot "your point of strength." Actors and singers are taught to project their voices from a place below their diaphragm. Regardless of where your exact "center" lies, the idea is to shift your attention out of your head and into the middle of your body.

To find your center point, inhale deeply into your belly. Then move your attention to the expanded spot near or just below your navel. While exhaling, keep your awareness on this spot. Let your awareness settle there for a minute as you become familiar with this part of yourself. Sports psychologist Tom Kubistant calls this activity "immersing."[13] He asks athletes to release all thoughts, tensions, and distractions by imagining there is an elevator in their heads that slowly moves down their bodies until it comes to rest inside their bellies. Then they imagine the elevator door opening but the contents are empty. After a few more breaths, they open their eyes but remain aware of the elevator. Their minds are now clear of all unwanted debris. Following Dr. Kubistant's guidelines, athletes learn how to stay in this state for long periods of time, which helps them perform at their best.

Once you are able to move your awareness out of your head and into your center, add a variety of activities to your practice. Play sports, listen to music, or hike while keeping a portion of your awareness on the center of your body. Try this for increasing periods of time. From this new perspective, you'll begin to see more details and hear finer gradations of sound. You can also practice centering when talking to someone else. You will listen more intently. Your responses will be more acute and sincere than when you formulated them in your head. If you begin to drift back into your brain, place one hand lightly on your tummy. This action brings your attention back into your body. Don't forget to breathe.

4. Focus

The fourth step after relaxing, detaching, and centering is to choose one word to affix in your brain to maintain yourself in the present. Most humans struggle with maintaining a clear mind; as an active high achiever, you struggle with keeping one point of focus even more than your less-active colleagues. To make matters worse, women have multimodal brains that are tailored for mental multitasking. Thoughts have a way of sneaking into your brain no matter what you do. Therefore, if you have one word to anchor on, you can keep the others at bay.

This could be the time to think of your keyword to call forth your vision. As I mentioned in chapter 4, I like to choose an emotion for my keyword. I focus on how I want myself and others to walk away feeling after an event or interaction. Consider what emotion you would like people to feel after being with you. Do you want people to feel happy, eager to take action, or inspired by your ideas? If you focus on one of these feelings, it's possible that you can pass this emotion on to the people you interact with. When you begin to lose your balance, you relax, detach, center, and regain your composure with your emotional keyword.

You can also focus on an archetype. Who do you want to be in this moment? What energy would best serve you in getting the outcome you desire? Focusing on how you want to feel or who you want to be helps you maintain control of your brain over a period of time.

BEING PRESENT BY HABIT

To take advantage of your windows of opportunity, use the four steps once or twice a day to be more conscious, aware, and present. As you train your brain to calm down and settle into the present moment, your practice will become a habit. You will naturally become more aware throughout the day. You will be amazed not only at the positive results you see when working with others but also with the clarity and contentment you will feel when you work in the present. Use these four steps the moment you recognize symptoms of stress in your body or as a tune-up before you address a group or engage in a conversation. You can use the four steps as a ritual to ground yourself before you do your ten-minute vision. You can Relax-Detach-Center-Focus at any time to ensure you are appreciating the splendor of a moment, not missing a second of your life. If you do, you are bound to see your windows of opportunity to explore, learn, and grow from your experiences.

You now are equipped for the voyage. You have identified the archetypal Circle of Selves. They stand ready to be called on when you need them. You've faced your myths of perfection. Daily, you will sharpen your vision to use as your weapon to reframe these myths when they appear. You have a four-step process to focus yourself in the present moment so you can capitalize on your windows of opportunity for learning. Finally, you know how to use journaling and Appreciative Dialogue to keep moving forward on your journey to your higher self.

You still need to determine your destination. The following chapter will help you identify what gives you a sense of purpose so you can make choices based on what you want instead of what you don't want. If you are like most Wander Women, you struggle with articulating your life's purpose.

Each time you think you have a handle on what gives meaning to your life, your purpose changes as you follow your wandering impulses. Chapter 6 will help you bring your purpose into focus so you won't lose your way no matter what turns you decide to take.

SIX

Choosing Your Course

What is the difference between high-achieving women and men? The most profound difference I have found is that high-achieving women change jobs and even industries more often than men. This statistic is even more important when you look at the differences men and women give for choosing to leave. None of the women in my study said they left a job or took on a new one based on a title or salary. They said titles and money were criteria in their selection, but paled in comparison to the possibility of doing meaningful work in their professional fields. The women all wanted to do something that had a major impact on the company or the world. Once they started a new job, as long as they felt they were making continual significant and unique contributions, they were inclined to stay with the company. If they didn't feel they were adding visible value with opportunities to try out new ideas, they moved on. If for some reason they had to stay in a job where they lost this sense of value, they felt as if they were suffocating. Whereas men are more likely to be wooed by position, power, and compensation, high-achieving women over the age of thirty are more attracted by the opportunity to be significant. If their work doesn't prove to be meaningful to them, they wander in search of their purpose.

Kelly, age thirty-nine, said, *"If my work doesn't give me a sense that I am doing something special, I'm not happy.*

That's when I feel most restless, when I get so busy that I lose an internal sense that what I'm doing is important beyond just my career and the profits of some company."

The problem lies in knowing how to define your purpose. Although you seek a sense of meaning from your work and you know what it feels like if this sense is missing, if you cannot articulate what makes you feel fulfilled you will have a hard time finding it in your work. What's worse, if you can't verbalize what you feel is most significant about your contribution, you leave the assessment of your value to other people's judgment. You end up relying on your clients or managers to tell you if your work is important and good. If you don't get this external validation, you either start looking for something else or you take on more projects looking for the one that will stand out. One of my clients said, "I take on so many projects I feel like I'm playing Whac-a-Mole. I keep pounding the mallet hoping to hit one of the moles on the head. I don't strategically whack, I just whack away. Every day at work, I whack away because every project seems important and I can't tell which one will win the prize."

If you depend on external validation to define your significance, you end up confusing your *desire to feel fulfilled* with your *need for recognition.* When people thank you for your contribution, you might think you feel fulfilled when you are just pleased that they noticed how much you know and how hard you worked. Not only will your pleasure be fleeting but you will find out that people are fickle when it comes to saying thanks. You might get a standing ovation from one group for your speech and the next day get only a few nods from a different audience. If you let a less-than-stellar evaluation steer you away from your life's work, it may take years before you rediscover what ignites your passion. Therefore, you shouldn't use applause, praise, or smiles to dictate your purpose. You need a consistent theme that serves to focus your energy regardless of other people's opinions.

In the extreme, your need for recognition is fueled by an irrepressible desire for fame, conscious or not. You see yourself talking with Oprah, speaking for a TED conference, answering calls for interviews, having your YouTube video go viral, receiving an award for your blog, or winning a reality show contest. Then if you taste fame once, you keep striving to recapture it, no matter what else shows up in your life to fulfill you. You are blinded by the chance at celebrity. Of course, there is always a possibility your name will be known by millions, especially with the reach of the Internet. The concern is that if your purpose rests on your fame, you may be chasing a remote dream for years without the ability to acknowledge what makes you feel incredible in the present.

This chapter will help you discover for yourself what gives you a sense of purpose distinct from your need for recognition. The gift of a sense of purpose is a feeling of contentment with your contribution in the present. You can find meaning in the moment instead of wishing for it in the future. Because "sensing" is based on an emotional reaction instead of a specific action, you will first determine what having a sense of purpose feels like to you. Then you can recognize what ignites these feelings. Once you identify what actions spark not just fulfillment but deep passion, you will be given the means to test whether your current situation is a roadblock or a step on your purposeful path. You will learn how to discern if your answers come from your own voice and or from your parents, peers, or society. From this place of knowing what is right for you, you can make better decisions for your career and your life. Your sense of purpose then becomes the guiding light that keeps you focused as you wander. When you passionately live with a strong sense of purpose, you can remember what is most important to you no matter how people judge you or what difficulties you face.

The greatest organizing factor of your life is to be able to answer the question, "For what purpose am I doing this?" Barack Obama, then a state senator, said in a 2004 interview, "I'm constantly asking myself questions about what I'm doing, why am I doing it." He explained, "The most powerful political moments for me come when I feel like my actions are aligned with a certain truth. I can feel it. When I'm talking to a group and I'm saying something truthful, I can feel a power that comes out of those statements that is different than when I'm just being glib or clever."[1] When you are clear about what you are meant to offer the world in a larger sense, you are better able to make in-the-moment decisions as well as significant life choices. Your sense of purpose gives you both the contentment and direction you've been missing.

ACTING VERSUS FEELING YOUR PURPOSE

I was taught an important lesson about the *distinction between declaring a definitive purpose* and *living with a sense of purpose* from a man in Kenya. Declaring a definitive purpose defines an action. The latter—living with a sense of purpose—identifies a feeling. I had always thought I was supposed to define my one specific life purpose if I were to be happy. A Maasai tribesman changed my mind.

After teaching a management class in Nairobi, I went on a three-day safari in the game preserve above the Serengeti. The training organizer had paid me for teaching partially in cash and the rest by giving me the trip. Because her travel agent cousin chose the trip without my input, I had no idea what going on a safari meant. I pictured nonstop trekking through forests and across the plains. Instead, I was given a small cabin to sleep in for three days outside of the game preserve. The cabin was part of a fenced compound with five other cabins and a lodge with a dining room and library. The owners drove tourist-filled Jeeps into the preserve to view the animals every morning from six to eight A.M. and every afternoon from four to around seven P.M. The animals slept in the heat of the day. From the lack of things to do in the camp between viewings, I surmised the camp managers expected humans to behave the same as the animals. The electricity was turned off after breakfast until three P.M. There were no phone lines and definitely no Internet connections. I couldn't go walking beyond the fences unless I enlisted a guide to shoot the animals, who might see me as their dinner. There was no way I could live with the guilt of killing an animal because I was unable to sit still, so walking was not an option.

I tolerated the first day by taking three naps in between finishing the two books I had brought along. On the second day, I went in search of something to do. I found a young man from the Maasai tribe digging a hole with a stick. I asked him if there was anything I could do to amuse myself in the confines of our camp. He pointed to a big shade tree. "The tree likes you to think about it," he said. "And if you sit under it, the cicadas will be quiet. They only make noise when they are lonely. You bring happiness to the cicadas and meaning to the tree when you sit under it. Do you have something better than that to do?" Because I had no good answer to his question, I sat under the tree.

The world became still around me. My mind cleared as well. I looked out on the vast plain below me. I felt small but yet a part of this timeless scene, as if I were standing on the spot where life began. I thought about my own endless quest for meaning, which felt trivial in light of the cycle of life that plays out on the African plains every day. Maybe the Maasai man knew the truth—I was meant to give purpose to the trees and keep the cicadas from feeling lonely. If this work gave me a sense of profound meaning in the moment, was I not living out my life's calling?

I sat without moving longer than I had ever sat before. I have no idea how much time passed. Finally my hunger urged me to move. I thanked my tree and promised the cicadas someone else would come by soon to keep them company. I passed my wise Maasai friend on my way to the dining room. He was happily giving his stick and the ground a purpose for being.

The incident taught me my life's purpose is more a feeling than a definition. Yet I still had to discover what would give me the same sense of purpose back home that I had sitting under that tree in Africa. You, too, must discover for yourself what gives you this sense of purpose. Laura Berman Fortgang asks in *The Little Book on Meaning*, "If our goal was to feel bliss, reverence, or love versus to achieve this or that marker of worldly success . . . how would that feel? How would the journey change?"[2] When you release the need to know the definitive answer to the purpose question, you live for a feeling instead of a goal. Fortgang says that when she started praying to know happiness, peace, and love instead of the answer to her questions around the purpose of her life, her meaning became clear. "That's the work," Fortgang says, "to get back to love."[3] We look too hard to find a unique, profound, and tangible reason for our existence. If the reason you seek a life purpose is to *feel* that you are doing what you are supposed to be doing with your life, then your quest for purpose should focus more on feeling than on doing. You should *seek to discover everything that makes you feel alive and connected* instead of searching for a specific role or action.

THE MEANING IN THE MOMENT

Therefore, instead of asking, "What is the purpose of my life?" you ask, "*What is the purpose of my work that inspires me in this moment?*" Whether you are running a marathon to help find a cure for cancer, reading a book to your child, or planning your meetings for the week, if the answer to the question, "for what purpose am I doing this?" makes you feel significant or fulfilled, you are living with a sense of purpose. The event can be as enduring as a ministry or as temporary as showing a new hire around the building. You may be driven to create a blog on leadership or to share your musical talents at a local coffeehouse. You might go on a retreat to reconnect with spirit or spend your spare time inventing gadgets that make life on earth a little easier. Maybe you see yourself as a bearer of laughter in a gloomy workplace or a storyteller intent on offering hope. Your light might shine on many or warm a single soul, be it the soul of a person, an animal, or an old shade tree. One purpose is no better than another. Whether your role at this moment is a sales director, a community organizer, an entertainer, a mother, or an engineer, *your purpose right now is whatever infuses you with the sense that you are providing a special gift that is important in the bigger picture of life.*

If your sense of purpose is nowhere to be found, then it makes sense to question if what you are doing is right for you. When I turned thirty, I was hired by a computer hardware company to produce technical training videos. Within two years, I was promoted to being the International Product Training Manager and traveled around the world teaching seminars to, and partying with, salespeople. Life was blissful. When I started the job, we were known for producing quality products. In the next two years, a string of bad management decisions resulted in a major drop in quality. I was told that it was up to me to keep the sales team motivated, a challenge I took on with great aplomb. Then one day as I was driving to work, a voice popped into my head screaming, "What are you doing?" As if a curtain had been pulled back, I could see that my momentary pleasures gave me no sense of purpose. Helping the salespeople was an excuse, not a purpose. I was making a good salary, getting recognition from above, and having fun, yet the products were bad. In the bigger scheme of things, I was doing more harm than good. Outside of work, my marriage was failing. I rarely saw my family and friends. From the moment I honestly answered the question, "For what purpose are you doing this?" I could no longer enjoy my work. I resigned shortly after. Yet without any guidance, I struggled when I tried to define what my purpose might be in a new job. I wandered through two other jobs before I could wake up feeling that my life was back on track.

Because the questions around your sense of purpose relate to what is going on in your world at a particular moment, what gives you a sense of connection to a larger purpose changes over time as life naturally changes. What fills your heart today may change next year. Carl Jung said, "But we cannot live the afternoon of life according to the programme of life's morning. . . . The afternoon of human life must also have a significance of its own and cannot be merely a pitiful appendage to life's morning."[4] Jung went on to say that if we do not shift our life purpose with age, we end up feeling worn out and unfulfilled regardless of the successes we earned at a younger age. Some shifts naturally occur based on the stages of life. Others are prompted by the broader perspective you gain with maturity. You may have once loved work that now feels stale. A friend of mine gave up his podiatry practice to do outdoor photography. The joy he felt earlier in his career had faded, especially because he felt his best work was hampered by the mandates of insurance companies. He found a new sense of connection while exploring a quiet wilderness. He says that sharing this beauty with others feels as profound today as the joy he once felt as a doctor.

Unfortunately, there is no way for you to know what will give you a sense of fulfillment in the future. Harvard psychology professor Daniel Gilbert explains why it is impossible to predict what will make you happy in his book *Stumbling on Happiness.*[5] Your brain is not equipped to correctly imagine the future. You cannot know what you will feel on your vacation, in your new job, or after you get married until you are there. Additionally, present feelings color your predictions. Gilbert says, "We cannot feel good about an imaginary future when we are busy feeling bad about an actual present."[6] In fact, Gilbert says, what you imagine will bring you joy in the future is generally a response to what is happening right now. If you change what you are doing, your prediction might change as well.

Therefore, the best you can do is *discover what gives you a sense of purpose, passion, and joy right now* and allow for the fact that what gives you these feelings *could be totally different later.* You have to keep asking yourself the question, "For what purpose am I doing this?" and allow the answer to come forward even if it is totally different from what you expected. The answer to this question, though it may change over time, will keep you centered as you wander. At least you will wander with purpose based on an understanding that your sense of purpose is *what makes you feel alive and connected right now.*

Keep asking yourself, "For what bigger purpose am I doing this?" to stay on track and happy. In 2002, I was hired to coach a woman who was facing difficulties in her role as an aviation manager at an airport in Arizona. She had been a senior aviation specialist with expertise in working with government agencies on compliance issues. In our first conversation, she explained that she took the management position because she thought it would give her more authority to do her job. Instead, she found that she spent most of her time handling disagreements in her team, nagging the less productive workers, communicating disheartening organizational messages, and trying to take up the slack for the members who left. She did not get along with her boss so she rarely asked for his help. To make matters worse, after the September 11 attacks on the United States, airport budgets were slashed and hiring was frozen. She could barely breathe for all the work she had to do. Motivating her team seemed like an impossible challenge.

I looked her in the eyes and asked, "Why do you work here?" She told me she loved aviation. This moment, of all times, was critical in terms of airport regulations. She knew how important her contribution would be. I asked again, "But why do you work *here*? You don't like your boss. Your team is falling apart. You have a passion for your work but it is smothered by your situation." She responded, "My passion for my work is second to my passion for being a grandmother. I live here because I'm close to my daughter and her two babies." I then asked her how many pictures of her family she had in her office. She had one or two in her desk drawer. I asked her to take a few dozen photos of her daughter and grandchildren and then have her favorites framed to hang on her office walls. In our next session, she told me that every time she felt she was losing her mind at work, she went into her office, closed the door, and looked at her pictures on the wall. Within moments, she felt full of energy, enough to go back out and face her challenges. She was now clear about how to answer the question, "For what greater purpose am I doing this?"

Be careful to differentiate what gives you meaning from what you feel obligated to do. When you are living with a sense of purpose, you should never feel you are making a sacrifice. You work should provide contentment, not resentment. If you don't have a passion for a task, you may be making a contribution to a greater good but it's not the type of work that will sustain your drive over time. As your contentment lags, so will your performance. For example, if you accepted a promotion but find you don't like managing people, your lack of sincerity will alienate instead of motivate your team. If you're writing a book to share your ideas but you don't like to write, the book will be a daunting process you may not complete. If you're caring for an ailing relative but you don't have a passion for nursing, your resentment may overpower your compassion. Although you are engaging in benevolent activities for good reasons, your purpose lies elsewhere. I'm not telling you to stop what you are doing. I just don't want you to be mad at yourself for not enjoying your work. Identify the passion you have for the grander purpose the current activity will help you fulfill. If you can't, know your purpose is still waiting to be found.

"HOMING IN" ON YOUR PURPOSE

In her book *Women Who Run with the Wolves*, Dr. Clarissa Pinkola Estés calls the act of looking inside to find what is important to you "homing."[7] A homing device, such as a metal detector, GPS, or a sensor that detects your car keys, is used to find something hidden from view. The tools you use to discover what purpose arouses your passion are also homing devices. The following exercise will help you unearth these feelings.

• •

EXERCISE: The Passion Quest

This exercise will help you to reconnect with what you are most passionate about in your life. You need at least thirty minutes in a comfortable, quiet place to adequately do this exercise. If possible, complete the steps with your dialogue partner. Speaking about your passions with someone who cares will enhance the effectiveness of this exercise as a "homing device." If you don't have a partner, take the time to explore the questions in your journal.

STEP 1

Quiet your logical brain by lighting up your emotional brain.

Choose and complete three of the following five requests.

1. Name the last movie you saw that you loved. Tell what you liked about the story. Share what you learned and what you will always remember.
2. Describe what you like about a book you are reading. Why do you find this interesting? What feelings or memories does the book stir up for you?
3. List three of your favorite smells. Describe what the smells remind you of.
4. Describe three of your favorite comfort foods and where you typically eat them. Explain why these foods are your favorites.
5. List three of your favorite sounds. Explore what you feel when you hear these sounds.

STEP 2

Now that you have activated your emotional center, dig into your long-term memory. *Choose and answer three of the following six questions.*

1. Describe one of the best days of your life so far. What happened that day that still makes you smile?
2. What would you like your first thought in the morning to be?
3. Recite your favorite saying or prayer.
4. Finish this sentence: "If I had a lot of money, I would . . ." After finishing the sentence, describe what you would do next if you were given even more money.
5. Finish this paragraph: "It is sometime in the future and CNN is calling me for an interview. I am excited about the opportunity to tell people about my success with . . ."
6. If a class were critiquing a movie about your life, what would you want them to say were the best parts?

After answering three questions, can you identify what triggers your passion today? Do you sense what you need to focus more on in your life to feel more passion? If you answered *yes* to these two questions, write down what you discovered and schedule a time to reflect on your answers. If you haven't yet discovered what stirs your heart, complete the next step.

STEP 3

Take your time in answering the following two questions.

1. What questions do you ask yourself when you are alone in your darkest moments? What steps can you take to bring what you ache for into the light?
2. What prison are you struggling to free yourself from? What will you do when you are free?

Now, declare what you are longing for. You may not be able to predict what will arouse your passion but you can sense what is important that is missing for you now.

• • • •

If you felt silly answering these questions, set the exercise aside but don't neglect it. Some people feel uncomfortable going into their emotional brain, especially if it has been a while since they ventured there. Many people numb their senses when they live in the thick of work in order to survive the barrage of stressors. Their protective brains then put up barriers, keeping them from feeling and then rationalizing this behavior by labeling these types of exercises as "touchy-feely." Yet I have used this exercise in classes of mostly male engineers and once with a woman on stage in front of an audience of four hundred people. Each time, when the reluctant participants relaxed and allowed their thoughts to venture into their "pleasure centers" in public, their mental censoring functions shut down. They shared laughter, tears, and breathtaking insights that deepened the discovery process for everyone in the room. If your brain stopped you from completing the exercise today, try it again when you can feel comfortable taking a journey through your mind. You will find a fascinating well of wisdom waiting to be tapped.

If you find that the exercise was fun but not particularly insightful, you may need to give yourself time for your passion to come into focus. Insights won't come when forced. Maybe you need to give purpose to a lovely shade tree and let the answers bubble up. Sometimes answers to your soulful questions show up when you least expect them, when you are shopping, playing with your children, or listening to a stranger complain. The contentment you will feel when you know what ignites your passion and what must be present for you to feel happy is worth the wait. If you can focus on what brings you passion in your busy, achievement-driven life, you will be able to sustain the transformation efforts you have started in this book.

After completing the steps in the Passion Quest, reflect on how your passions relate to the work you are doing. Be sure to write down what you discover in your journal. Your perspective may change over time as you work on your self-awareness and development. It is good to have a running account of the changes. The Purpose Test is an exercise for discovering if there is a way to connect a difficult task to your passion.

• •

✎ **EXERCISE:** The Purpose Test

Consider a current situation where you are struggling for motivation and focus. Write in your journal or tell your dialogue partner all the reasons for doing the work.

- Which of your reasons for doing the task feel like "shoulds"?
- What, if anything, inspires you about the task or the outcome?

Try to organize your attention around the second question. If you are still struggling, look at experiences in your past that have stirred your passion. Can you relate those experiences to your present challenge? For example, if you love developing your team members but have to fire someone, can you see how your actions will honor the hard work by others on your team and possibly help the person you have to fire to find more meaningful work? Can you push past the administrative work of a project by focusing on what excites you about the possible outcome? Can you cope with your difficult boss long enough to get the skills and knowledge you need to ensure the success of your next adventure? Can you stay with an exercise schedule knowing this will help you live long enough to dance at your grandchild's wedding? Center yourself by asking, "What greater purpose am I serving?" Your relationship to the activity should change when you sense the meaning in the motions you are making. If you can't, then it could be time to move on. You have better things to do.

• • • •

DON'T MISS THE TURN SIGNALS

Once you discover what gives you a sense of purpose, periodically ask your heart if what you once defined as meaningful still feels fulfilling. "Has my purpose changed shape over time? Am I leaning in a slightly different direction? Is there a stirring in my soul that tells me I have work to do somewhere else?" As you learn and grow, what gives you a sense of meaning will most likely change. You should ask yourself these questions on a regular basis or your restlessness may send you off on a new path for all the wrong reasons. When you wake up in the morning, ask your heart if all is well. When you're sitting in the dentist's waiting room, ask your heart. When you're driving home in traffic, ask your heart. You may be studiously checking off tasks in your daily planner while your soul has turned on your turn signal. Before you become disappointed or frustrated with life, determine whether you can realign your work with what feels purposeful. If you can't, then use your new sense of purpose to guide you in your search for what's next.

Left to its own devices, your vocal, logical brain is not inclined to choose inspiration and love over society's markers of success. You have to dig deeper and ask your passion what to do. Your passion can help you make the right choices if you ask and listen. To take the purposeful path, you have to *feel* what is right for you in your bones, your gut, your heart, and your soul. Once you know this, it will be easier to balance your archetypes, vision joyful days of work, and maximize your windows of opportunity. In Part III, you'll learn how to apply what you have learned so far to help you stay on track as you navigate your journey at work.

PART III

Wandering on Purpose

SEVEN

Maintaining the Momentum

Making the decision to transform yourself is easy; sustaining your commitment to fully realize your transformation is not easy. Changing habitual behavior patterns can take months of focused awareness, experimentation, and reflection. At times, when you are giving up old ways of being to try on new selves, you will feel as though you are driving through a patch of fog on the freeway. When you can't see where you are going, you get frustrated by not knowing what choices you should make. Your brain tells you to take the first off-ramp and head back to where you came from. There is safety going back to old thinking and behaviors, especially the ones that served you well in the past. Yet if you stay the course, the road will eventually reappear. Your world will forever look different from this point of view. This chapter will give you the tools you need to help you honor your commitment to transform.

Transformation starts with an ending. In the second part of this book, you started the first phase of transformation by recognizing what assumptions you need to quit believing so that you can move toward having more contentment and a sense of direction. Even though these beliefs served you in the past, you need to let them go to move on. The first phase of your transformation required you to say good-bye to who you were so that the work you do to bring in new beliefs, identities, and behaviors has a chance to take hold.

The first phase prepares you for the second phase of

transformation, the most difficult part of your journey. The work you have done so far has shifted your thinking, which in turn affects how you approach your work and your relationships. If you want these new beliefs and behavioral patterns to become permanent, there are still a few things you need to know and do. According to William Bridges in his book *Transitions: Making Sense of Life's Changes*, the transformation process has three phases: endings, the neutral zone, and beginnings.[1] The second phase you are now entering, the neutral zone, is where the view gets foggy.[2] You've separated from the past but haven't yet assimilated the new you. Your brain is in the process of weakening old connections and strengthening new ones, but the new wiring hasn't fully set. You have to go through a rite of passage before you can relax and feel natural with the changes.

When you first try out a new behavior, it may feel awkward and inauthentic. The gap between the old and the new way of being feels uncomfortable. You aren't sure who you are or what you are supposed to do. If you don't understand what is going on in phase two, you may either think something is wrong with you or surmise that doing this work was a dumb idea. Either way, you may abort your commitment to change.

If you quit the transformation process prematurely, not only will you compromise your goals, but you will also lose a fabulous chance to experience what it feels like to stand in the state of pure possibility. In his classic anthropology book, *The Forest of Symbols*, Victor Turner describes the second phase of transformation as the "liminal period," when new configurations of ideas and self-concepts can emerge.[3] What feels awkward is actually your brain going through the repatterning process. In other words, your discomfort is essentially a signal of positive growth. This is the best time to experiment and reflect. When you are unsure of yourself, you should "embrace the mystery" with curiosity instead of distress. If you can see that life is about making changes and it is better to flow with the unsteadiness of the transition, you will be in a better mental place to accept the unknown. The more you open your mind, the more options become available. As Turner said, you have the chance to enter a state of "pure possibility."[4] When you accept instead of resist what you are feeling in phase two, you ease the transition into the third phase, beginnings.

The three phases of transformation aren't linear, so you have to diligently monitor your progress during the process. Some changes happen quickly, moving you into a new beginning right away. Then you get so mired in your work you neglect your visioning and dialogue sessions, so the old way of thinking returns. Or the changes you are trying to make feel awkward when interacting with others, so you give up. Therefore, it is vital you pay attention to what is going on in your brain for at least a month, more if possible, to stop yourself from reverting to your old thinking patterns and rationalizations partway through the process.

At times your upbringing may appear as the voice in your head, questioning the value of the excessive amount of self-focused work. For example, you might be frustrated with the pace of change because you were probably brought up to believe that when faced with a problem, competent people figure out what to do and "just do it." This belief runs counter to taking the time you need to observe yourself, test new ways of being, reflect on the effects of your trials, and then talk about different possibilities before you fully claim a new sense of self. You can't "just be it." You must recommit to staying the course many times in the process.

It is easier to live with bad habits than to change them. Many medical studies confirm that most people who start health regimens give up and return to old habits without constant support and frequent evidence of the positive results of their efforts. Even when your decision to change makes perfect sense and you've decided you want the results enough to work for them, you may fall back into destructive behavior without certain tools to help you maintain your commitment.

DEPLOY YOUR WEAPONS

This chapter will give you four tools, or weapons, to help you overcome your tendency to find other things to do than the work of transformation: (1) powerful emotions; (2) positive evidence of success; (3) a community of support; and (4) the frequent reawakening of your sense of purpose. The transformation process can be likened to the hero's journey, or, for our purposes, the Heroine's Journey. The basic structure of this age-old narrative pattern starts with the main character venturing forth from her normal world into a region of supernatural forces that challenge her wits and bravery. When she returns from this adventure, she has both riches and wisdom to share with others.[5] As the heroine of your journey, you leave behind what is known only to face demons and surprises before you realize you have everything within your power to complete the journey successfully. The journey takes a massive amount of courage and focused determination. You don't just shift into a confident new you. You have to be honest with yourself, which can be painful. You have to try out less than perfect behaviors, which can be distressful. You have to ask for support and assistance, which can feel uncomfortably vulnerable. These are the monsters you face before you find comfort in your new definitions of self and success. Then once you integrate these new distinctions, it may not be long before your restless nature will urge you to go on another journey. You may go on many journeys in a lifetime.

Yet the greatest obstacle on your journey is the crushing amount of information you have to deal with, which shifts you into survival mode and threatens your resolve to transform. The average knowledge worker spends more than half her day rushing through e-mails and text messages, answering phone calls, sifting through pages, and listening to gossip whether she cares to or not, trying to find time to work on her priorities. According to the research firm Basex, nearly 30 percent of your workday is lost to uninvited interruptions.[6] The moment you feel overwhelmed, you forget about your commitment to changing and revert to old behaviors. This is when I hear the justification, "I am who I am, so what." Your brain has a program titled, "Who I think I am" that it prefers to play over and over, especially when you are under pressure.

You cannot fully control how your day plays out, yet you can influence the outcome by being present and taking the specific actions outlined in this chapter to sustain the changes you initiate no matter what pops up. These actions will help you continually choose to be the self you have envisioned. You already know how to rally your energies to meet the challenge of new accomplishments. *Now it's time to challenge yourself to live the examined life.* The key to taking on this challenge is to, in every moment, consciously choose to stick with your plan.

The following four tools are your essential weapons for sustaining change whether you are facing internal demons or external demands coming at you from all directions. Additionally, the tools will enhance the process by helping you recognize the possibilities that arise in the neutral zone, making the experience more enjoyable than difficult. As a result of following these suggestions, you will increase the number of PEAK experiences you have to draw from in your appreciative dialogues.

The PEAK Transformation Tools

1. **P**ick your emotions.
2. **E**valuate your evidence.
3. **A**ccept support.
4. **K**now your sense of purpose.

The first three tools are activities you can begin today. You learned the fourth tool in the last chapter: how to get in touch with your passion and sense of purpose. This chapter will show you how to use this sense of purpose as a "pick-me-up" when you come dangerously close to halting your journey mid-stream.

1. Pick Your Emotions

Both positive and negative emotions play a role in the success of your transformation. When you opened this book, you probably had a desire to feel something more, whether it was more passion, contentment, joy, pride, or the peace of mind that comes with better understanding yourself. Yet the impetus to continue reading the book and completing the exercises was more likely based on your deep desire to decrease stress, regrets, anxiety, sadness, or an unclear longing in your gut. Your emotions have a significant impact on your judgment. They influence every decision you make regarding change. The intensity of your desire to change, whether based on a positive or negative emotion, correlates to the likelihood you will complete the process. You have to want the change badly enough to overcome the discomfort, boredom, confusion, embarrassment, and worry that pops up to stop you along the way.

You must allow yourself to feel a strong emotion, with anger being one of your strongest motivators, before you fully commit to making a complex change in your self-concept and behavior. An intense negative reaction to your circumstances revs up your internal motor more powerfully than a lightly held wish. Through extensive research, Jennifer Lerner and her team at the Harvard Decision Science Laboratory found that anger both encourages people to believe they can control their future and then motivates them to take risks.[7] Many times I have asked a client, "Are you finally mad enough at yourself for allowing this to happen again?" The question focuses the anger on their own avoidance mechanisms, disarming the blocks they had for changing. When you adamantly say, "Enough," you may be angry about your circumstances but probably you are just as angry at yourself for standing in the mud with two good feet.

The skill is to shift the focus of your anger away from external circumstances to instead focus on what you strongly desire to change within yourself. It is not your flaky boss or overwhelming responsibilities that make you scream at strangers while you drive. You should be angry that it has taken so long for you to realize that you have the power to change your circumstances. If you then channel the energy of your discontent toward doing the intentional transformation exercises that you learned in Part II of this book, you will be using your anger to initiate the positive shifts you need to change your life. You must shift internally before you can change your external reality. Anger can be a great mobilizer of positive action.

However, sustained anger can be destructive physically in your body and externally in the world around you. Anger, frustration, stress, and the other negative emotions that trigger the brain to release adrenaline and cortisol will over time wear out your body by causing high blood pressure, heart disease, ulcers, hormonal imbalances, a weakened immune system, and a host of digestive problems.[8] Also, anger can eventually drive away the result you want. You can drive people away with your anger, people who could help you achieve your goals. Brain researchers are substantiating the effect of one person feeling irate or vengeful on others in the vicinity, whether the angry person displays or suppresses these emotions.[9] Even if you don't direct your emotions at others, the measurable energy your emotions emit repels people, counteracting your desire to connect with people in a new, more positive way.

Therefore, once you commit to your transformation journey, you should shift your focus away from what is missing in your life to what you want to passionately and positively create. Determine what you want to end and then make the shift from a negative to a positive expression of your passion. You still need powerful emotions to sustain the process. Adamantly wanting something to end is a good way to kick-start the transformation process. Yet once you are off and running, you need a positive obsession to sustain your efforts long after you close this book.

• •

EXERCISE: Giving Voice to Your Emotions

Timothy Wilson said in his book *Strangers to Ourselves* that if you can discover the "story of why" you can better overcome your rationalizations to discover what is truly at the source of your emotions and reactions.[10] After you experience anger, disappointment, or disgust, discover "why" by asking yourself:

- What do I feel I have lost?
- What do I feel I should have?
- What are people not giving me that I deserve?
- What am I doing to keep myself small?

Ask yourself how badly you want what you deserve and what you are capable of creating:

- What do I want more of in my life?
- What is my heart telling me to do? *(Do the Passion Quest in chapter 6 to help find the answer.)*
- How can I shift my devotion to what I dearly want to create?

• • • •

Put your emotions in service of what you desire. Employ positive, powerful emotions to help you survive your Heroine's Journey. Remember to fire them up every day as you vision, test out, and dialogue about your goals.

2. *Evaluate Your Evidence*

Although emotions have a hand in creating your reality, you must compose easily attainable goals to give your brain the evidence that what you want is attainable. As I mentioned earlier, the brain will revert back to old habits if the change you are trying to make feels too uncomfortable. To counteract the discomfort, you need to frequently experience the feel-good payoff for your personal development work. From the moment you make the choice to change, you must biweekly if not daily recognize both the effort and positive effects of your work. For example, you can choose to be peaceful instead of irritated today. Yet to transform this choice into a long-lasting behavioral change, you need to (1) see early and consistent evidence that you can be successful at letting go of feeling irritated, and (2) tangibly evaluate the evidence as a positive experience when you journal or dialogue about what happened.

In order to evaluate your evidence, you have to be very clear on what behaviors you want to create in addition to the habits you want to release. Remember that your brain doesn't comprehend the word "don't." You have to focus on what you want to create as evidence of success, not on what you don't want to happen anymore.

For example, one of my clients, whom I will call Barbara, made a commitment to change but nothing happened until she identified the archetypes and specific leadership behaviors she wanted to focus on instead. Barbara was a regional sales director for a major pharmaceutical company who had just been given a new territory to manage when she hired me to coach her. Her priority was to ease off her work schedule to create more time for her personal life. She was hoping to marry her boyfriend and have children, yet she was feeling overwhelmed by her new responsibility. After our first coaching session, she agreed that she needed to quit thinking she needed to know everything about the products and territories assigned to her team. This meant she had to tightly schedule her research time. She agreed to vision her changes and journal about her successes between our sessions.

Weeks went by without her making any changes in her schedule. When she started postponing our sessions, I asked her to set aside a special hour where we could review her archetypes in order to explore who she was being when she was making decisions. During this session, Barbara declared her primary archetype to be the Detective because she based her significance on knowing more than everyone else. She loved when people came to her for answers even though this meant many interruptions in her day. Before I asked her to choose another archetype to balance this energy, I asked her to recall a peak experience where she was honored for her leadership capabilities instead of her ability to inform. She described delivering a difficult performance review where, in the end, her employee thanked Barbara for being honest but caring. She had sensed that part of her employee's problem was based on a lack of downtime and self care. Barbara suddenly took in a deep breath, smiled, and said, "Funny how I saw in her the exact same problem I am now facing." When looking at her own imbalance, Barbara decided that being a model of leadership meant modeling the life she wanted for her employees. She then chose to call forth the energy of the Lover archetype to remind herself of the importance of caring for people instead of worrying about how much they appreciated her. She wanted to open her heart to being a developer of her employees, not just being their data support. In our next session, she shared her new model of leadership with me, which focused on creating venues where her managers shared information with each other instead of always having to come to her.

With more clarity about what she wanted to create, Barbara designed little goals each day so she could walk smoothly and positively into her new identity. In evaluating the results of her goals, she realized the world wouldn't crash around her if she went on a mini-vacation without her computer. She didn't lose respect when she used the words, "I'm not sure. I can't wait to hear what answer you find." She celebrated when one of her top performers was promoted to manager because this gave her a new opportunity to hire and develop someone new. She acknowledged each win in a brief e-mail to me. Each time she recognized a major breakthrough, she rewarded herself with a new novel she committed to read, a romantic dinner with her boyfriend, or a decadent pedicure, which further acknowledged that she could enjoy her fabulous life without being seen as an incompetent leader. By the end of our nine-month coaching engagement, not only had Barbara found more joy in her life, but also the assessment ratings of her leadership capability had soared. Her brain finally accepted that she didn't need to know everything to be a great leader.

In short, your second tool to help you sustain change is to regularly identify, document, and acknowledge the evidence that you can successfully enact your vision. When you repeatedly glean and appreciate what is positive about your actions, you give reality a chance to unfold before your eyes. You are less likely to get frustrated when change doesn't happen as fast as you would like and when unforeseen events force a change in your plans. The more times you acknowledge the good effects of your efforts, the more you will flow with what you can't control.

First, make sure you have defined specific activities you can celebrate. Then create an action plan that you can weave, piece-by-piece, into your daily visions. Write about your victories in your journal. Talk about them with your dialogue partner. Send congratulations notes to yourself. Predetermine rewards and then give them to yourself to validate your progress. The transformation is more likely to stay on track if you make a point of noticing your accomplishments every day. Then, little by little, your goals become habits. Eventually, you become the person you vision yourself to be.

3. Accept Support

Whether you work with a coach or not, you want to amass a group of women going through a similar growth process to yours. Coming together with like-minded women will keep you from feeling isolated. Empathetic, encouraging friends committed to growth can help one another maintain focus even when layoffs loom, employees whine, the kids at home scream, health issues nag, and projects overwhelm. If you can find other women who are consciously trying to become better leaders or live more satisfying, purposeful lives, you can develop personal connections and create communities with women who regularly help one another learn and grow.

Unfortunately many people still believe that women do not support one another at work. I argue that since their confidence has grown, women don't feel the need to protect their turf as much as they used to. Most of the women I coach are generous with their advice and support. The younger the women are, the more they were brought up using the Internet and know the value of networking. I believe catfights, gossip mongering, and backstabbing have decreased. Then someone tells me a horror story of how one woman derailed another woman's career and I begin to question my own research. Executive coach Peggy Klaus noted in a *New York Times* article in 2009 that women young and old, up and down the ladder, still engage in subtle bullying by limiting access to important meetings and committees; withholding information, assignments, and promotions; and blocking the way to mentors and higher-ups.[11] Although women may more readily bond with other women at work, it appears they still define their own tribal boundaries. You may incur the anger or indignation of your female colleagues if you fall outside of this tribal definition and become a threat to their goals. The effect of these behaviors destroys relationships. Trust is hard to rebuild after even one offensive act.

No matter why this behavior is still happening, you need to rise above it and find the women who honor their female friendships because of all the benefits that female bonding provides. I coach female executives in a number of large-scale corporate initiatives focused on growing their promotable women. The most successful of these programs provide more than coaching. They create opportunities for their top-talent women to network. They recognize the need for women to support one another both professionally and personally in addition to getting mentoring and coaching. In 2002, a landmark study was completed at the University of California, Los Angeles that found that one of the best ways for a woman to combat stress is to call a friend.[12] Dr. Laura Klein, one of the study's authors, says, "it seems that when the hormone oxytocin is released as part of the stress response in women, it buffers the 'fight or flight' response and encourages her to tend children and gather with other women. When she actually engages in tending or befriending, more oxytocin is released, which further counters stress and produces a calming effect."[13] In other words, if you are feeling stressed, find another woman to bond with over a cup of coffee. Your conversation will more than help you resolve your problems; the connection will increase your feelings of calm and contentment.

Though often neglected, your friendships are a great source of strength while you are on your Heroine's Journey. Putting friendships on the back burner when you get overly busy with work and family is one of the greatest mistakes of busy, working women. According to Malcolm Gladwell in his book *Outliers*, successful people do not make it on their own: "no one—not rock stars, not professional athletes, not software billionaires, and not even geniuses—ever makes it alone."[14] Your friends not only open doors and connect you with other people, but they also can dialogue with you and sometimes just be silent with you as you come to understand what you are encountering on your quest. You need coaches, mentors, and communities of support to provide sounding boards and critical eyes to help you stay on track. The time you spend with these people is as important as the time you spend on your work. There is no need to "tough it out on your own." Asking for help is a sign of strength, not weakness. If you are truly committed to creating amazing results that impact your workplace and beyond, then you need to access the wisdom and support of others. Gathering a community of support is not a luxury you can put off until you have time someday. Establishing and maintaining your network is a critical step in your growth process.

Creating Your Communities

If you don't have a formal community of support among women committed to growth in your company, you can assemble a community from women in your external networks. Look for like-minded women in your professional associations, in executive development classes at your local universities and colleges, and even in your gym classes. One of my clients, the regional vice president of human resources for a large financial institution, asked her hairdresser to recommend female executives from other professions who might want to join her community of support. As a result, she found six other women who welcomed the chance to meet once a month to discuss their goals, obstacles, options, and next steps. They ended each meeting celebrating both large and small wins that each woman experienced the month before. This forced my client to keep a tally of her wins, the evidence she needed to stay on course. She also found the women were quick to show up or call when one member had a family tragedy. She doesn't have a support group; she has a loving community of friends who are committed to helping one another thrive professionally and personally.

When I decided to transition from working as an inside corporate trainer into an independent speaker and trainer, I joined a group of seven other trainers looking to redefine themselves in the same way. The group was called G.I.F.T.—Giving Ideas Freely Together. Formally, we met monthly to solve one another's problems, share resources, and celebrate successes. Yet even more important, we were each just an e-mail or phone call away. Working for yourself can be a lonely experience, especially if you spent years working inside companies surrounded by people before you ventured out on your own. G.I.F.T. was incredibly important to me the first few years I was in business for myself. We added four members over the years; each of the current members had a deciding vote before accepting a new member. Three members went back to work inside corporations but remained members of the group for the camaraderie. The group stayed together for five years, gifting one another in many ways.

It is crucial to be clear about your selection criteria for inviting women into your network, for both formal communities and informal friendships. Choose women with positive outlooks who are willing to accept help as well as offer it; who will commit to showing up physically and mentally when you schedule time together; and who are on their own personal development journeys. When you find a woman who seems to fit your criteria, ask her to have coffee or a meal with you. If a woman only talks about herself, she won't be interested in supporting you and your colleagues. Some high achievers have a strategic mindset when they meet someone new, meaning they will be intent on impressing you with their genius and on discovering how you can be of service to them. Instead, look for women who inspire you to trust them through their spontaneity, their authenticity, and their willingness to share their own concerns and dreams while having a sincere desire to hear yours.

Also, make sure you have at least one woman in your network who will be honest and compassionately direct with you even when you don't ask for her opinions. Find someone who will not back down when you adamantly defend yourself. Having at least one person who is willing to be direct and honest with you in a benevolent way is critical for your growth.

If you find a woman you think would be a good fit for one of your formal communities, you and your colleagues should be clear about the steps you should take before anyone extends an invitation to someone new. Everyone should feel safe to reveal what they are thinking and feeling in the meetings. Therefore, everyone has to meet potential candidates and have a say in who should join. You may want to pre-screen a candidate with your group before you extend an invitation so you can see if your colleagues also think the woman will be a good fit for the group. Then, when you find someone you think might be a great addition to your group, during your next conversation bring up the idea of meeting your community and see how open she is to the idea. Don't be offended if she declines your invitation. Her time and commitments are as precious as yours. She might be a good friend for you but not a joiner of groups.

As you nurture relationships in your community, which includes both formal groups and informal friendships, don't fall into your habit of only offering and not accepting support. Another myth you were brought up to believe is, "I can figure everything out by myself." You are the antithesis of the needy girl. Therefore, when you start asking for help, you might feel awkward and strained. You will have to override your mental programming around asking for help, which can be a struggle for you. The intensity of this struggle will be amplified by the nature of your cultural upbringing. For example, saving face among both men and women makes it extremely difficult for people of Asian cultures to admit to mistakes or limitations. A few years ago, I was asked to administer an emotional intelligence test to a team of economists in India. Even though I attempted to give each person private feedback, none of them wanted to hear their own results. They kept interrupting me with questions about how their scores ranked in comparison with their colleagues, which I could not tell them. They also wanted to know if the test could be culturally deficient because they did not earn perfect scores, even though I clearly explained that perfection was not a human option. They may have taken my suggestions to heart but I wouldn't bet on it based on our conversations. They were too focused on being the best to hear anything else. If you cannot receive feedback from the women in your community, they will stop asking you for your ideas.

In addition to your cultural upbringing, be honest about your own professional boundaries about whom you will accept help from. I have observed that the higher men and women climb in their fields, the less open they are to receiving help from anyone inside their companies and possibly inside their industries. Executives refuse to go to training classes. Many of them will only accept coaching from a few select names. Stanford professor Robert Sapolsky found that many scientists spend more time protecting their old discoveries than considering new ideas.[15] Through other studies, he surmised that the more we age and gather expertise, the more selective we become regarding whom we will listen to. The question you need to ask yourself and others is, "Whose suggestions are you willing to receive?" If you struggle with asking for help from others in your company, would you be willing to accept support from other women in your field? How about listening to women in other professions? Be honest with yourself before you expend the energy to gather your community of support.

Then consider that the women you ask may also have certain boundaries.

When it comes to your acquaintances, even your long-term friends, you want to regularly consider if the relationship you have with them continues to be beneficial for both of you. If you find that a friend is spending more time expounding about her never-ending dramas and complaining about her circumstances, you may need to step back from the relationship. *Better to love her from a distance than to resent her up close.* You can understand her suffering, but if the relationship brings out the worst in you, it isn't healthy for you or her. This separation is critical for your own development. Be honest and firm about the amount of positive energy you need in your life. You must surround yourself with women who are committed to strengthening their self-care, who enjoy Appreciative Dialogues, who are willing to admit they aren't perfect, and who are confident enough to ask for what they need so they can move forward with their lives.

Finally, to be able to accept support from other women, you need to be conscious about your own dominant emotional state when talking so you can accept, not deflect, their advice. Since you launched your journey with a strong emotion, often anger, you may not notice when it is time to soften your strong "will to power." Your expression of passion can be overwhelming. For others to feel safe enough to offer you help, you have to emotionally invite them into your space and show acceptance and gratitude for their suggestions. Practice your four-step presencing routine (outlined in chapter 5) before you meet by relaxing, detaching, centering, and focusing on how much you care for and respect your colleagues when you are with them no matter how passionate you are about the topic of discussion. If you don't like their advice, you can still appreciate their intentions. Say thank you. Refrain from using the word "but," which negates their suggestions. If you have to, just say "interesting perspective" and move on. You are better off doing what you can to preserve the relationship instead of protecting your ego.

• •

EXERCISE: Creating Ground Rules for Communities of Support

To build trust in your formal communities of support, establish some basic ground rules. Use the following list to start the discussion about agreements and then modify the list together so it is meaningful for your group.

Everyone should be able to say the following statements to each member of the community.

1. *I believe that you want the best for me in all of my endeavors.* You will openly share resources and ideas. I will graciously accept your suggestions.
2. *I believe that you won't judge me based on second-hand information.* If you hear someone saying negative things about me, you will vow to check this out with me before you accept the statements as truth.
3. *I believe that you won't talk negatively about me to others.* If we have a problem, you will come to me to talk about it. If you have to sort out the issue with someone else first, you will come to me shortly after and let me know who you talked to first so there are no surprises.
4. *If I have a problem with you, I will ask to speak to you privately soon after the offense occurred.* I will then:
   - Get clear about what you did that made me feel the way I do.
   - Listen to your perspective and try to understand what you meant.
   - Work toward an agreement with you about how we will handle these situations in the future.

• • • •

I attribute much of my success over the past thirty years to the power of my friendships. They have helped me to overcome addiction, live through divorce, grieve the loss of my parents, re-create my life more than once, and achieve my grand goals. My communities have changed over the years, though some of my friends have stayed with me through it all. I feel very fortunate to have many powerful, compassionate, humorous, generous, and courageous women in my life. In mobile societies like mine where neighbors tend to be strangers, communities of choice are more essential to happiness than ever before.

4. *Know Your Sense of Purpose*

Alfred Adler, one of the founding fathers of psychoanalysis, felt that mental health depended on having a life purpose focused on the greater good. A key theme that runs through much of his work is the need to develop social interest based on a sincere "community feeling."[16] He focused on the word *feeling* as I did in chapter 6 to differentiate the sense of purpose from specific actions. Whatever gives you the sense that you are a part of something bigger than yourself is essential to your happiness and your ability to expand your self-concept. Lacking a sense of purpose drains your joy and stresses your mental health.[17]

Therefore, your fourth weapon is to use your sense of purpose to keep your head above the chaos. It is not the magnitude of your purpose that will calm your soul. It is the value you believe you are giving in the moment and the recognition that what you offer is "enough" even though you are hell-bent on accomplishing grand goals.

For example, I once left a workshop early to make sure I got through the Friday afternoon security line at an airport in Washington, D.C., in time to catch my flight home. I had not been home for more than a day in three weeks. I was looking forward to spending the weekend quietly unpacking, answering my mail, and enjoying the company of my boyfriend. When I got to the gate, people were swarming around the agent because the flight was delayed. Anyone who had to make a connection, including me, might need to find another flight or spend the night somewhere other than home. The closer I got to the desk, the louder the disgruntled passengers were screaming. Adrenaline surged through my blood: if I didn't make my demands known, I might be stuck in Washington. I maneuvered my way toward the front of the crowd. I ignored complaints, feeling I had the right to be pushy. When I got to the desk, I heard the agent say, "I'm doing my best, sir. We have the list. If we can find you a connection, we will." At that moment, I knew his pain was greater than mine. As I slipped my ticket onto the counter, I said, "It must be very difficult helping people when all they want to do is scream at you." A wave of relief washed over his face as he smiled and then turned back to the irritated man in front of him. My body relaxed as well. I would either go home that night or first thing in the morning. In the big scheme of things, losing a few hours at home mattered much less compared to the gift I gave the agent. When I remembered how good it makes me feel when I help people cope with adversity, I knew what I had to say to the ticket agent. My words connected us both to a sense of peace that allowed us to go with the flow of what life was dishing out at that moment.

When you know that even your smile, a kind word, or your willingness to listen is a part of your noble purpose, you will know what it feels like to be "in alignment" with yourself and the world around you. You can feel contentment in your restlessness. You can channel your passion so that it is constantly renewed and you won't burn out. This is the life energy you need to sustain the journey.

In the next chapter, you will look at three scenarios for applying what you have learned in this book. Whether you want a promotion, seek fun new challenges, or prefer to create an entirely new game plan, chapter 8 will bring together all the elements in this book to illuminate what your Heroine's Journey will look like. The tips you learn in the chapter will help you create your personalized map. Remember that once you are in transit, you need to regularly deploy your weapons: choose a powerful set of emotions to fuel your drive; gather the evidence of your success; find your community of support; and act with your sense of purpose to keep you on track. Even if your journey is delayed, you will be able to stay the course of transformation.

EIGHT

Navigating Through, Below, or Away from the Glass

When it comes to making important career decisions, many of my female clients start our coaching relationship by saying, "I'm not sure I want to be vice president" or "If I'm going to be CEO, it might as well be for my own company." Are they giving up? On the surface, you would think these women would fight for top leadership positions regardless of the difficulties. They love a good challenge. They like visibility and recognition. They prefer leading rather than being told what to do. They want to make a significant contribution that provides meaning for their employees as well as for themselves. If they were coached to see the options available to them more clearly, would they make different career decisions? Even when they decide that leaving is the best choice, they still need to identify where they want to go next and how to get there. Helping my clients verbalize their frustrations and desires often leads them to different conclusions and action plans from what they brought to our first conversation.

To help you make more thorough decisions when you plot out your career, this chapter will present three scenarios for you to consider. In the first story, Lee clearly defines the reasons why she wants a promotion and then conceives a plan to earn an executive position. The second story shares how Gabrielle plotted a path of continual challenges and recognition while staying below the glass ceiling. The third story follows Kerry as she tests out her options before making the decision to start her own business. Following these stories, I'll give you tips for imagining your future if you, too, determine it's time to move on. Each woman used various exercises from this book to check out the validity of her assumptions and beliefs, to see through the eyes of different archetypes for guidance, to create visions, to dialogue about peak experiences, and to look for the path that best inspired her sense of purpose. I share these stories in hopes that whether you choose to navigate within your company or out on your own, you move forward with clear intentions for what you want for your future.

LEE THE LEADER

Lee chose me to coach her after receiving a leadership ranking that placed her in the middle of the pack among her peers, indicating that upper management felt it would take years for her to be ready to take on a senior leadership position. When we started coaching, Lee was a middle manager who held the title of Director of Customer Relationships, Western Division but dreamed about the good she could do for the company if she held a vice president position. To determine what led to her mediocre ranking, we looked at her assessment ratings and I interviewed her manager and human resources representative. Looking at the comments on her 360-degree performance review, it appeared that her team of customer service managers enjoyed working for her. They said she included them in decision-making, frequently checked in with them to make sure their needs were met, and engaged them through relevant challenges on both an individual and a team level that were fun as well as constructive.

Yet Lee's activities went unnoticed by any leaders beyond her boss. Her HR representative told me that she wasn't on anyone's list of people to watch for promotion potential. Her work was appreciated but not revered. She had never participated in a large corporate project and most of the executives wouldn't know her if they walked by her. Lee thought she was entitled to promotions because of her team's success when in fact no one else, not even her boss, made this connection. Her boss loved her performance but said she lacked leadership presence. From her 360-degree performance review, her peers saw her as contentious and lacking emotional intelligence.

Before we set our sights on her goal, I coached Lee to determine if her desire to be promoted was based on her needs or on her passion. She agreed that the title would be an ego boost. Yet she also felt she would be able to accomplish so much more for herself and the company if she were in a position of greater authority. If given the chance, she knew she could have a powerful impact on the success of the organization by better engaging all company employees in the goal of delighting their customers. She felt most alive when she energized others. She wanted the chance to meet this challenge.

After comparing her desires to the opinions of her leaders, she defined three coaching objectives:

1. Manage up to her boss and beyond so that her name was always mentioned in conversations about future leaders in the company.
2. Manage sideways to develop a network of internal support among her peers.
3. Manage her communication habits so she could do more of what worked and less of what was hurting her.

Managing Up

Lee had to learn how to manage up so that upper management would know her name and invite her into their ranks. Like most of today's high-achieving women, she did not need lessons in assertiveness. She knew how to speak up when she had an idea or opinion. Yet what good was having a strong voice if she didn't have a stage to speak from? She needed to make her abilities and accomplishments known so her name would come up in succession planning conversations. She needed face time to promote herself and her ideas not only to her boss, but also to the management team above him. In short, she needed to determine how to create positive visibility.

Before she could take any real steps, Lee decided the first thing she had to do was to adjust her attitude from being angry at management to feeling determined, even passionate, about helping them and the company to excel. She was mad about the decision the assessment team made stating she was years away from being ready for a promotion. Although her anger provided her with a strong emotional launch for change—the "I'll show you" factor—she would have to shift her emotions from anger to her determination for being a powerful leader of change. She didn't want to be seen by management as an angry Rebel. She wanted to be seen as a committed Visionary who gets results. Yet, while we were exploring how she could do this, she blurted out, "They're mostly a bunch of men with old ideas. They should be asking me for my ideas instead of me groveling to them." When I asked her how this perspective served her, she sighed and admitted it was a problem she needed to fix. To help her, I asked her how she defined managing up. She said that she had always believed it was about playing a negative political game. I asked her, "From your perspective as a Visionary, how would you define managing up?" After exploring the conversations about the future she would love to have with the leaders, she redefined managing up as her way of *creating a positive conspiracy for change*. Her strategy would be to gather support one-by-one for high-return projects. When the senior managers saw how well she could orchestrate creative solutions with great results, she would be able to sell her bigger ideas to people willing to listen. She loved the idea of creating a positive conspiracy. By reframing the title of her vision, she could honestly say she was working to find ways to cooperate with people who had the same overall objective of success as her own. With this mindset, she could proceed minus the chip on her shoulder with a more positive tone.

Next, she discovered that the best way to connect with upper management was to approach them with a solution to one of their most pressing problems. She decided she wanted the three vice presidents of sales, operations, and logistics to know what she was capable of doing. To do this, Lee had to call on her Detective archetype to find out what was perplexing the people she wanted to know better. Lee's expertise was in customer service. She was aware of some of the problems in sales, operations, and logistics from listening to customer complaints. To better understand the problems in these three areas, she gathered her team of managers to help her brainstorm the possible sources of the problems. After compiling a comprehensive list of possible sources, she asked her team what front-line managers they knew in those areas who could verify the details and importance of the problems. Lee contacted the managers her team suggested. She found that everyone she approached was more than willing to talk about their problems and why they felt these problems existed. With this information, she chose three problems to focus on, one for sales, one for operations, and one for logistics.

Lee then crafted a pitch for each of the VPs explaining how her department could work with theirs to find an innovative solution to their particular problem. She sent an invitation by e-mail to the VPs of logistics and operations to join her for lunch to discuss a possible project. Lee drummed up the courage to give her invitation in person to the VP of sales because she would be in a meeting with her at headquarters in a week. All three people accepted her invitations. At lunch, the VP of operations listened to her pitch, agreed that her ideas were good, promised to get back to her, and then never did. However, the VP of logistics loved her suggestions and asked her to help create a task force to implement her ideas. Finally, she had such a good connection with the VP of sales during their lunch meeting that Lee asked her to be her mentor. The VP was so impressed by Lee's initiative that she suggested they meet for coffee for half an hour each week. Lee came to each session prepared with a topic to discuss and a willingness to listen. After a few weeks, it was clear that the relationship was mutual because Lee had built a bridge between their two departments. Mentoring also gave Lee even more insight on whom she needed as her allies in the company and what she could do to get better visibility among the leaders. Eleven months after we started coaching, Lee was promoted to Regional Vice President. She felt her problem-solving work on the task force with logistics and her ongoing relationship with sales clinched the promotion.

One of the keys to managing up is to make sure you include your boss in your plans and don't do anything that could be considered as going behind your boss's back. First, be sure that you meet your boss's priorities before you start focusing elsewhere. Consider offering solutions to your boss's most pressing problem before you present your ideas for helping out other departments. Then start by asking your boss, "Would you support my efforts in creating wider visibility in the organization?" Once you get a yes to this request, say, "I have a few ideas about working with some other departments that I know will help improve our results as well. The results should also help your efforts at enhancing the reputation of our department." Then share your ideas in detail. Your boss might have a perspective that you missed in your planning. Remember to document your conversation with your boss so no one forgets the details of your agreement. Internal career progress requires that you manage your own boss successfully.

Managing Sideways

If your peers name you as the person they most admire and want to learn from, you will likely be seen as the person with the most leadership potential when succession is considered. A study was done by two leadership instructors, Jack and Carol Weber, at the University of Virginia's Darden School to determine which rater group—manager, direct reports, or peers—was the most significant predictor of promotability. The Webers followed the careers of managers who were participants of their executive development program and had taken a 360-degree feedback assessment while in school.[1] The peer reviews from these assessments won out as the greatest predictor of future promotions.

The purpose for earning the respect of your peers is not to win a popularity contest but to successfully achieve your goals. Your peers will either bolster or hinder your attempts to move forward. They can generously offer assistance or underhandedly sabotage your projects. Also, your employees want you to work well with your peers so you are better able to negotiate for resources and remove barriers that stand in the way of getting their work done on time and most efficiently. Executive coach Scott Eblin calls the failure to look to your left and your right to your team of peers a bad case of "tunnel vision."[2] The higher you climb, the more you need to establish collaborative relationships with your colleagues to succeed.

Lee was a good manager, but she had not been using her strength of inclusiveness to manage her relationships with her peers. I asked Lee, "If your manager left and your team got to vote on who they wanted to be their leader, would your peers elect you to the position?" She said probably not. The dismal ratings from her peers on her review suggested the same conclusion. She humbly admitted to "hogging the limelight." She loved being the star, which could overshadow those around her. Even more damaging, when we looked at the three assumptions that create the mindset of perfection—*I am always right*, *everything is up to me*, and *I will always be disappointed*—she owned up to all three beliefs, which naturally distanced her from her colleagues. Her attitude was smug, which probably seeped out in her nonverbal gestures. Because she performed well as a manager, I asked her, "What management strength do you possess that you could use with your peers to earn their votes for you as their leader?" When she answered "inclusiveness," I asked her what specific activities she could do to be more inclusive with her peers. In addition to showing them more respect, she said she would take more interest in their projects and look for ways to help them solve their most pressing issues as she was going to do with her boss. Becoming an advocate for their needs would make her a valuable ally. This meant she had to listen to them more in meetings. She also decided to set up individual meetings with them to better understand their goals and issues. Hopefully, these meetings would also serve to rebuild any trust she had broken in the past.

I then approached the subject of how her peers described her as competitive instead of cooperative. When I asked her to describe the competitiveness her peers accused her of, she laughed and said she only competed with herself. Yet when we reviewed the goals she had made so far, she still stood in the superior role of offering, not asking for help. She really wanted to be accepted by her peers. Again with humility, Lee admitted that she needed to "get over herself" and acknowledge the competencies and experience her peers brought to the table. They did not see her as their Queen. They saw her as the enemy. We talked about the many ways she could become a Collaborator with her peers, which started with asking for and respecting their ideas.

In the end, Lee said that if she were truly focused on improving the bottom line, she needed to be relationship-focused as well as results-focused in her conversations with her peers. She agreed to sincerely ask her peers for their feedback as well as ideas, including their evaluation of her leadership presence. We explored how vulnerability is actually viewed as a strength of leadership. She also determined to praise her peers more for their ideas, effort, and results. She vowed to do a ten-minute vision every morning that included successful interactions with her peers. She would also log her successes every evening. Finally, she agreed to have a coaching session focused on how she could manage her emotions and reactions in her meetings, which we called "Managing your mouth."

Managing Your Mouth

With her plans for managing up and sideways in place, Lee turned to her communication style, specifically to her listening skills. She determined that saying less could be an advantage. She admitted to overselling her ideas, and that she always felt she needed to explain everything to be understood. If her peers and boss really were competent, then she was probably spending too much time stating the obvious. To manage her mouth, she set the goal of practicing "stop and think" before speaking. She would then ask herself if listening were the better choice at that moment. To further her effectiveness, I suggested she use the "Stop and WAIT" exercise. She loved WAIT, knowing instinctively that the exercise would help her be much more influential in meetings.

• •

EXERCISE in WAITing

Before you speak or if you find yourself pontificating when other people are not engaged, stop yourself and ask: **WAIT**—

Why
Am
I
Talking?

> If you have a good reason for talking, continue. If you only have a good rationalization, turn your attention to someone else and ask for their ideas. Remember, "The less I say, the more profound I am."

• • • •

In order for Lee to change her speaking-to-listening ratio, she would also have to manage her emotions when speaking to others. If she got excited or frustrated in a meeting, she promised to breathe, center, and count to three before responding. To be truly emotionally intelligent, she would reflect on the source of her emotional reactions after the meeting was over. She could then determine if she needed to have a private meeting with someone to discuss what she felt had been overlooked. Yet in the meeting, she would Relax-Detach-Center-and-Focus on her emotional as well as verbal choices.

In short, Lee was learning how to strategically communicate. Aristotle said, "Anyone can become angry—that is easy . . . but to do this to the right person, to the right extent, at the right time, with the right motive, and in the right way, that is not for everyone, nor is it easy."[3] When you can evaluate a situation in such a way that you see options in how you can react and then carefully choose when to speak up, when to ask questions, and when to listen for more information, you are being a strategic communicator. It is important to choose your battles. It is also important to choose when to calmly absorb what is going on around you so you will have more weapons if you need them in the future.

This led to us tackling Lee's most difficult habit of always fighting for what she felt was right. I shared with her an experience I had with my boss. I was complaining to him about a colleague's lack of support for my grand idea when he took my hand, patted it, and said, "Dear, you can quit fighting now. You've made it." I yanked my hand away from him. He quickly added, "I know fighting helped you get where you are today. Now it's time you learn how to truly connect with and persuade others to see your point of view." Though I disliked his condescending behavior, the truth of his words hit me squarely between the eyes. That's when I learned the difference between being a strong woman and a woman of strength and influence.

There is a difference between being strong-willed and being seen as powerful. Many high-achieving women take the "pit bull" approach to be heard, to right the wrongs they see, and to earn recognition for their brilliance. Yet as a "woman of strength," you speak to be heard in a different way. You can still draw your lines in the sand. You can still speak with passion. Yet you will focus on presenting the merits of your ideas instead of bashing someone else's. You will even look where your ideas intersect with an opposing approach to create alignment instead of competition. The opposite of weak is not brutish. If you want people to see you as powerful, you need to cultivate your ability to listen, to honor other people's ideas, and then to speak your vision in a way that also addresses their needs. Instead of being seen as a fighter, you want to be seen as model of reason, compassion, determination, and, of course, good humor.

A Strong Woman Versus a Woman of Strength

A strong woman shows her muscle . . . a woman of strength shows her confidence.

A strong woman isn't afraid of anything . . . a woman of strength admits her fears and then models the courage she wants others to carry.

A strong woman won't let anyone get the best of her . . . a woman of strength freely gives away the best of what she knows.

A strong woman avoids making mistakes . . . a woman of strength realizes life's mistakes are great lessons to learn from.

A strong woman looks forward to showing her prowess on the journey . . . a woman of strength has faith that while on the journey, she will truly become powerful and wise.

Finally, Lee made plans to maintain her goals in three ways: (1) reflecting on her experiences in her journal; (2) creating three-minute visions to set her mind straight each morning; and (3) identifying a dialogue partner for weekly chats. First she planned to spend at least fifteen minutes at the end of each day thinking about her progress and, in particular, noting when her efforts were successful. She used her successful actions as the input for her second commitment, creating a daily visioning routine. Third, she identified one of her peers, the director of sales support, to ask to be her dialogue partner. She had wanted to deepen her relationship with the director because it seemed as though they were on a similar path. A week later, Lee called me with the news that her peer was excited about the chance to work with her on developing their careers together. Lee's transformation had shifted into high gear, which led to the promotion she wanted . . . and beyond.

THE ADVENTURES OF GABRIELLE

The second story features Gabrielle, who preferred the freedom she felt she had navigating below the glass in a middle-management position. Maybe she would choose to be an executive someday, but for now she felt more passionate playing in the middle. She liked the flexibility she had to balance her joys outside of work with her accomplishments inside. She worked for a large hospital corporation so there was opportunity to move around the company if she found positions that interested her. To date, she had earned two promotions and one lateral move in the four years she worked for the company. Her performance reviews were always excellent. Her relationships with her peers and the four people she managed were good. Her goals were to garner desirable assignments, continue to get recognition, earn generous raises, and maintain a say in what her future looked like without getting stale in any one job. Yet she knew management generally wanted top talent to focus on promotions. She didn't want them to think she wasn't committed to the company or to her own improvement. She just wanted to shine below the glass ceiling for now. Therefore, Gabrielle's coaching objectives included:

1. Develop her eye for projects that would have a significant impact on productivity and give her visibility in the company. The goal was to become indispensable so she could maintain her political power without having to move up the ladder.
2. Find champions in the senior ranks to sponsor her projects.
3. Create small tests of her ideas before presenting proposals for corporate consideration.

Developing an Eye for Hot Issues and Projects

Most high achievers see things from a *tactical perspective*, meaning you focus on how to do your own work better or on how your direct reports can be more productive. You are always asking, "What needs to get done?" Whereas many people wait to be told what to do, you look for what is the *right thing to do right now* for you and your team. Although you are proactive about improvements, you tend to be fixated on what action is needed now rather than on seeing what hot issues are emerging in your company or your industry.

The skill you need to develop is to evaluate your work

from a *strategic perspective*. This means stepping back and researching what trends are emerging and what issues will need to be addressed six to twelve months from now based on what changes are going on in your company, industry, marketplace, or the world. Claire Shipman and Katty Kay describe this focus in their book *Womenomics* as finding the high-profile, high-reward projects that are just starting to grab everyone's attention. "If you are ahead of the curve on buzz, it also gives you a chance to leap on those areas early on and claim them as yours," say Shipman and Kay. "It makes you and your boss look good, which helps everyone."[4] A strategic focus helps you stand out.

You can broaden your perspective to include strategic as well as tactical thinking by trying to uncover the new ideas people are talking about in your field. You can monitor and act on the trends that are forming by listening to what the executives are talking about, reading the industry newsletters, tapping into bloggers who write about your industry, joining discussion groups on social media platforms, and doing Internet searches on topics that keep coming up. What's new and needed in your world? Survey the broader landscape to find what's next that you can wrap your passion and energy around. This makes you a *perceiver* as well as an *achiever*.

You can also use strategic thinking to analyze your actions before you leap into a task that puts you on the cutting edge of operational practices. Let's look at the difference in tactical and strategic thinking with an example of creating a new budget for an upcoming project.[5] If you think *tactically as an achiever*, you might review a few formats before choosing one you think will work best. If you think *strategically as a perceiver*, you first step back to explore the many ways the budget will be used so you can create something that will meet needs as they arise instead of having to make many changes along the way. Find the answers to these questions, "What purposes will the budget serve? How will it be used?

Who needs to see it? What platforms for sharing will work best? Where can I locate the latest best practices in creating and displaying this type of budget? What people can I get to help me make the best decision?" After integrating all good ideas as best you can, you propose your solution to all the stakeholders to get their buy-in and, hopefully, their admiration.

ACHIEVER		PERCEIVER
Tactical thinking	→	Strategic thinking
What can I do?		What possibilities can I see?

Unfortunately, many factors keep you thinking tactically instead of strategically. First, because you like seeing immediate results, you don't think you have time to do research. Second, too many choices can be confusing. Third, it takes courage to propose out-of-the-box solutions that you aren't sure will succeed. The answer to the first roadblock is to make scheduling time for research a priority. The second roadblock requires you to clearly define your decision-making criteria up front so you don't get lost in the sea of choices. You can bolster your courage to face the third roadblock by finding champions for your projects and organizing tiny pilots for your ideas before you roll them out. Gabrielle decided she wanted to propose more out-of-the-box solutions, so we focused our coaching on the next two goals, finding champions and organizing test runs.

Finding Champions

In order to get buy-in for your new project or for the new position you want to create for yourself, you will need to find an executive who will plead your case with other leaders when the time comes. Look for an executive who has a reputation for supporting new and often unconventional ideas. Also, look for someone who will benefit from what you want to try. If you can demonstrate how your ideas will increase your champion's efficiency, productivity, or image of success in the company, you will have his or her ear.

For example, when I was the training manager for a semiconductor manufacturer, I found a champion in a rising star in the organization. He had requested a team-building course for the department he managed. Instead of granting his request, I took a strategic perspective to help him explore the root of the problem and other possibilities that might be more effective in getting the results he wanted. I offered some ideas I learned at a conference I had attended on trends in training in our industry. He ended up realigning his teams into cross-functional problem-solving units, removing the silo structure they had been in. We then provided the training and coaching for his managers to make the transition a success. When other departments started inquiring about what he had done, he then championed my work with other leaders until we eventually engaged the CEO to support a new team structure across the organization. My job expanded from corporate training to organizational development, which was infinitely more rewarding for me.

To solicit someone to be your champion for a change you want to initiate, you might start by asking this person to mentor you as you attempt to test out and sell your ideas. Suggest a time frame for your meetings and what you would like to gain from the relationship. For example, you could say, "I would like your guidance on a project I'm intending to introduce into the company. Could we meet for thirty minutes twice a month for the next three months so I can get your opinions and suggestions?" Gaining advice and encouragement from someone who knows how to "work the system" in your organization will help you sidestep barriers and avoid making unnecessary mistakes. When the time comes that you need resources and approvals beyond what your own boss can give, your mentor is likely to become your champion in other divisions and at higher levels. However, don't keep your boss in the dark. Let your boss know early on that you have sought a mentor in the organization.

Create Small Tests Before Going Global

Instead of launching a major change program just because you believe it will be a good idea, design a couple of low-cost, low-risk experiments that will prove your point. This way, you will have more than a theory to use when you face resistance to your ideas; you will have real data to use to support your proposal. You might start with your own team or gain support from a peer to try out a new idea with both of your teams. If you don't need a lot of money, you probably don't need to justify your actions to anyone in advance. For example, you might try out a new problem-solving technique, an innovative way to develop products, an out-of-the box customer-support process, or a system for project team members to communicate using a Wiki and an internal Twitter program.

Start by writing a clear and compelling vision. If you want people to try something new, be clear about the results you are looking for so everyone understands what you expect to happen and why your idea is a good thing for them. Visioning also helps to measure the actual results against your expectations so you can clean up your mistakes before trying your idea out on a larger scale. If successful, these ideas can lead you to expand your current role within the company. You might be able to create a new position for yourself if you demonstrate real value for the organization.

The book *The Future of Management* recounts the case study of how Jeff Severts transformed sales forecasting in Best Buy, demonstrating how someone can view a process strategically to uncover a needed innovation, enroll a champion, and then use small tests to demonstrate the value of his ideas.[6] In 2004, Severts managed consumer and brand marketing for Best Buy. However, he found that his success depended on the reliability of the eight buyers who made up the sales forecasting team. Severts was not in a position to question the forecasting system directly, yet he felt there had to be a better way to accurately forecast sales. After attending a workshop that focused on how to use the "wisdom of crowds" to make important decisions, Severts came up with an idea to improve forecasting by asking store sales associates to weigh in with their opinions. Before he attempted a trial, he engaged an executive champion who promised to bring his idea to top management if his idea proved successful. Severts actually carried out two tests, one to forecast a month of gift card sales in a few stores and then a bigger test to forecast an entire holiday season in a region. Both times, the sales associations out-forecasted the management team. With the help of his executive champion, he presented his results to top management, who then gave him a budget to tap into the wisdom of the sales associates across the country. By taking a strategic perspective, engaging a champion, and starting out small, Severts not only increased the odds of his own success, but he also changed the way his company does business.

Gabrielle's goals for navigating below the glass represent a new way to "have it all."[7] Although it can take some heavy negotiations to get the challenging high-profile assignments while saying "no" to the career ladder, you can wander inside a company for many years without losing steam. As a high achiever, you are a valuable resource. This means you can leverage your value when you stake out the position you want, even if the title and responsibilities you want don't exist today. When more and more companies realize they are losing their best women because of corporate inflexibility, you will have more opportunities to create your own path in the organization, earning rewards on your terms instead of by following the traditional, vertical corporate tracks. Be creative, keep pushing the envelope, and create raving fans in your organization. If you do this, you can choose whatever direction you want to take.

KERRY'S BIG DREAM

During my first coaching session with Kerry, she was so angry about being passed up for a promotion that I could barely insert the words "I see" and "I understand" into our conversation. One of Kerry's male peers had been promoted to research director. Kerry was livid because the division vice president had promised she was next in line for a promotion. As she relayed her story, every other sentence ended with, "I should just quit." I carefully listened for Kerry's perception of the situation between her emotional outbursts.

My intention was to differentiate the facts from her assumptions once she calmed down. We both had to see the reality of the situation clearly before I could coach her on what would be the most beneficial next steps for her to take. When she finally ran out of steam, I asked Kerry, "What do you know to be absolutely true about this situation?" We whittled down her complaints to two major facts: (1) Bob had been promoted instead of her; and (2) the divisional vice president had promised her a promotion nine months ago but had said very little about the possibility since then. She speculated about the reason for the betrayal, about the lack of support from her immediate boss, and how the archaic culture of her organization played into the results. However, the two facts were the only ones she could substantiate. Based on this clarification, Kerry agreed her coaching goals should be to:

1. Identify the truth about her potential in the organization. Then if she still chose to leave . . .

2. Clarify her vision of her future so she could begin preparing for the move today.
3. Determine what it would take to stay motivated while preparing to leave.

Determining the Truth: Rational Versus Emotional Career Decisions

Most of the women in my research based their career decisions more on what they didn't want in their lives than on what options they wanted for themselves in the future. They tended to leave jobs after they grew bored with the work, after they were overlooked for a title or assignment they thought they deserved, or after their ideas and desires were ignored. On this note, I have been hired many times to coach women who have already decided to make a career change. They are mentally done with their current boss or organization. Most want to leave right away and want help figuring out their next move. Their decisions to leave were based on emotions, not on a plan. They were disappointed, angry, and determined to find a more appreciative workplace. Occasionally I get a client like Kerry who hasn't fully made up her mind to leave. She was crouching down, preparing to jump. Thankfully, she called me before leaping.

To help Kerry paint a holistic picture of her best options going forward, we spent the first month defining the reality of her current situation. Even though her peer had been promoted, she needed to determine if all doors to promotions were closed to her or just that one. First, she looked within her own department. She promised to question people about her leadership potential with no emotion and to accept their perceptions with no reactions. This was not the time to fight for herself. This was the time to uncover the truth. She went to both her boss and a manager in a related division and asked them to outline what they felt it would take for her to be promoted to the next level of leadership. Unfortunately, neither meeting was fulfilling. Her boss never answered her directly. When she pressed him for details, he gave her a general, patronizing compliment and complained about his own inability to plan for the future. She evaluated his behavior as unsupportive of her growth in the company. The manager of the other department gave her even less hope.

I then asked Kerry to step back and evaluate her promotability in general in her organization. Do they tend to send more men to leadership development programs? Is there a balance of gender in top leadership positions? Are there women on the board of directors? She said she intuitively knew the answers but was surprised that she had not gauged her success from this perspective when she first hired on. I told her many women today ignore the fact that discrimination still exists in both obvious and subtle forms. I didn't want to discourage her. I just wanted her to evaluate what was true for her organization so she could make a logical instead of an emotional decision. In this case, Kerry was right about the lack of leadership opportunities for her in her company. With that in mind, she chose to start planning her future and, more specifically, her exit.

Preparing for the Move

Once you've made your decision to leap, preparation is critical. Although you are smart and committed, if you jump into action without sufficient preparation you will be running for months to catch up. The more you can prepare yourself for your new life—including changes in your schedule, your working environment, your relationships, and your use of time for both work and leisure—the better you can slip into your new lifestyle.

First, you want to imagine as best you can what your new life will look like. Although the reality might prove to be different, this picture should inspire you to move forward. What about your new life stirs your passion and fills you with a sense of purpose? Talk to people who are leading the life you would like to have. Ask them what their normal workday looks like. Get specific. Ask them what productivity tools and time-management techniques they use. Ask them to share one thing they wish they had known before they started on their current path. Look for social media groups of people in your new industry. Join in on their discussions. See your new life through their eyes. You can't hold the entire picture in your hands, but you can start piecing together the puzzle so you feel more prepared when the day comes to move on.

To help you draw the picture of your future day at work, fill out the Life Areas Assessment.[8] The Life Areas are pieces of the puzzle to help you build the picture of your perfect workday in the future. Consider aspects of your personal life as well as work so nothing gets left behind.

Once you complete the chart, write out a narrative of what you think your life will look like in one year from the date of your exit. What would make this workday perfect? You can include two or more days in your story for variety. When I left my corporate job to start my own business, I envisioned what my perfect week would look like when my business was one year old. I set aside two days to coach one-on-one, two days to train and speak, and a buffer day for administrative and marketing tasks. Within each day, I exercised and spent some time connecting with family and friends. It actually took me two years to settle into this schedule. Then as the nature of my work shifted into more speaking, training, and writing, I had to shift my life accordingly, making sure I didn't compromise my commitment to my health and friendships. To honor my commitments, I redo the assessment annually. Work has a way of taking over my life when I'm not looking.

Include what you like now and what you would be doing if you were more satisfied with your life areas. Write more of what you like to do and less of what you'd rather

LIFE AREAS ASSESSMENT

Life Areas	How does this look in my life today?	What can I picture for my new life?	What will I commit to starting/ stopping/ continuing?
Work/Career			
Job Tasks			
Communications			
Atmosphere			
Location			
Resources			
Health			
Exercise			
Diet			
Relationships			
Parents			
Primary/Spouse			
Children			
Siblings			
Friends			
Co-workers			
Manager			
Customers			
Home Living Space			
Atmosphere			
Aesthetics			
Location			
Learning			
Career Growth			
Personal Growth			
Emotional Health			
Life outlook			
Relaxation			
Self-Reflection			
Spiritual/Religious			
Finances			
Expenses			
Savings			
Leisure Time			
Hobbies/Sports			
Vacations			
Volunteering			

not do. Define who you are when your needs are met and when your work highlights your strengths and passion. Include your favorite archetypes. Describe your best work relationships. Add in time for reflection and dialogue with a coach or friend. Include details such as the clothes you wear, the equipment you use to conduct your work, and the car you drive. Don't settle for what is happening today unless it is perfect as is. Picture your ideal. If you have difficulty with this exercise, try describing what you don't like and use opposing words. For example, if you think your current boss is a control freak, picture what it would look like if you had a boss who trusted and respected you. If your mornings are too rushed, picture yourself preparing in a more leisurely fashion and then listening to inspiring music in your car on the way to work. Don't get hung up on how you will make everything happen. Let your dreams flow. Making the changes comes later. Stick to the *who*, *what*, and *where.* Worrying about *how* this will happen at this point will only muddy the stream of ideas.

Once you can picture your future, you can start breaking it down into goals. Ask yourself:

1. What can I start doing today to ease my transition?
2. What about my new work life can I begin to integrate into my current work?
3. Who can I ask to support me in making my transition?
4. What do I need to do to stay committed to my choices?

I used this imagining exercise in a workshop for women making life transitions. After composing her story, one of the participants said, "What I had been hoping for was stuck in my head and not clear. Now my dreams have come alive." A good resource to help you reinvent your life in a year is Cheryl Richardson's book *Life Makeovers: 52 Practical & Inspiring Ways to Improve Your Life One Week at a Time.*[9]

Maintaining Motivation for the Present in Light of the Future

The third challenge Kerry needed to tackle was to avoid feeling like a lame duck at work once she made the decision to leave. This is a universal problem that you, too, will experience whenever you tell yourself it is time to move on from any position or relationship. Although planning a new move is inspirational, the more you plan the more you are distancing yourself from your current work. Your mind is focused on the possibilities the future holds, not the present. Your mind wants to justify the move by negatively judging the people you work with and the decisions the leaders make. You fixate on the worst aspects of your job. Everything bugs you. You are likely to feel too tired to work by midday. On the other hand, you might also start second-guessing your choice to leave. When you worry, you are also focused on the future, not the present.

You have to choose to feel connected each moment so your thoughts, your joy, and your creativity don't drift away with your daydreams. Practice centering yourself in the present moment as you did in chapter 5. At various times throughout the day, observe your stream of thinking and note what emotions you are feeling. Don't judge yourself when you find your brain has wandered. Instead, acknowledge the rumblings of change going on in your mind and body. Then choose to return to the present because it is an important step on your journey. Ask yourself, "What can I do to see my current job as building the platform for my leap to somewhere else? How is this moment going to help me in the future?" Your current job is still a laboratory for learning. Find the lesson today that will help make your life easier tomorrow.

To help you stay present, try changing your routines to force yourself to think about what you are doing instead of counting the minutes until you can go. If you have traveled to work every day on the same route, take another one. If you have a grooming routine for your hair and make-up, mix it up so you do things in a different order. At work, start your day with a discussion on a current event instead of checking your e-mail. Find people you never got to know well and see what you can discover about their lives. Miss a meeting. Attend someone else's meeting. Practice conversations you may have in your next job. Study how your company makes its brand known, which may spark ideas for yourself in your next position. Call in the energies of the Explorer archetype. See each day as an adventure full of surprises to be discovered. The time until your next adventure will fly by.

Whether you decide to climb the corporate ladder, navigate below the glass, or take the leap into a new job or career, you are only choosing to take one more step in your life's journey. Then next year, you can stay on your path or choose again. When I published my first book, I asked my coach how much time and money I should put into my marketing efforts. He said, "Whatever you choose, remember that this is not the one big thing in your life. This book is just one step. You may publish other books or you may choose an entirely new direction. They will all be steps that take you to the next big thing." Adding to his words, I say—you will not know what the biggest thing in your life is until you near the end of your life and look back. Every step is a big deal worthy of your passion. And every step leads to the next big deal. Enjoy the lessons and the pleasures each moment has to offer and every decision you make will be perfect.

NINE

Raising the Flag

Many of the women I meet tell me they wish the leaders they work for would see the light, that the contribution of high-achieving women is vital to the economic health of their organizations. Therefore, the structure and rules that define the company culture must change to meet the needs of their top-performing women. You have two options: (1) you can pray that your leaders will find and read the articles that support your point of view or (2) you can fuel the changes yourself. I'm sure you will agree that the first option is less likely to make a difference than the second. If you do not feel comfortable raising the flag directly, this chapter presents a letter for you to copy and send to the relevant leaders in your organization. You are welcome to customize the letter to fit your needs. If you are willing to advocate more actively for change in your organization, Chapter 10 will provide you with ideas for making your voice for change heard by your managers and executives.

A copy of this letter is available at www.WanderWomanBook.com. Please feel free to forward the page to any executive who would benefit from the message, or copy and customize the letter to fit your communication style and the needs of your organization.

• • •

From: Concerned Employee
Re: Organization Structure
Thank you for taking a moment out of your busy day to read my letter. I want to share with you a solution to a problem our company is facing. I offer these ideas in the spirit of improving our productivity. Please take my comments and suggestions as a sign of my dedication to our success in this fast-changing world.

Have you read the news about the effect that female leaders are having on business and economic success? Studies in the United States, Great Britain, and France have proven that companies with women composing at least one-third of their leadership team make more money.[1] In these countries, the more women on a company's senior management team, the less its share price fell in 2008 during the economic downturn. In another study that spanned the last nineteen years, Pepperdine University found that the Fortune 500 companies with the best record of promoting women outperformed their competitors by anywhere from 41 to 116 percent.[2] McKinsey also reported data in a global study indicating a significant increase in the financial performance of companies that have at least a third of their senior management team consisting of women than those organizations with few or no women at the top.[3] A report released by Ernst & Young in the World Economic Forum in 2009, *Groundbreakers: Using the Strength of Women to Rebuild the Global Economy*, shared research that pointed to the need to capitalize on the contributions women make as leaders, entrepreneurs, and employees when moving the world's businesses and economies forward.[4]

You would think these studies would prompt companies to hire and develop top-talent women, but the reverse has proven to be true. A 2009 study of 376 organizations worldwide found that 50 percent more men than women get special attention, including mentoring and attending "high-potential programs" designed to boost their careers and transition them into higher-level jobs.[5] To compensate for the lack of women in senior positions, some companies provide special programs to develop women to be leaders. Unfortunately, many of these programs are designed more to "fix" the women than to develop them.[6] They focus on improving communication skills and giving them tips on how to better cope with the work-life imbalance they have to live with. Few provide the advanced business skills the women need to be successful in the ranks of the global executive.

The result—instead of fighting to achieve high-level positions, the women are leaving in droves. In 2004, the Center for Work-Life Policy asked 2,443 working women with graduate or professional degrees how their careers were progressing.[7] Nearly 40 percent said they were planning to leave their jobs to either further their education or make a career change, which included starting their own businesses. Fifty-two percent of the women with MBAs said they were planning to leave because they found their work was no longer enjoyable or satisfying. Many said they didn't feel valued and they lacked a sense of purpose. So they decided the best thing would be to move on. They did not lose their ambition. They no longer felt they fit in or they didn't want to fit in with what they saw.

Did you know that there is a talent shortage looming? In the next few years, half of the baby boomers will have retired, leaving millions of positions requiring college degrees to be filled. That gap will keep getting bigger. Highly educated employees will be in huge demand. Guess which sex now earns more college and advanced degrees?[8] No matter if the economy is up or down, if you want to fill positions with the best possible candidates and then engage their loyalty so they stay with you in the long run, you need to pay attention to what women want from your company.

I've taken the time to research what other companies are doing to attract and retain high-achieving women. Companies such as Deloitte, GlaxoSmithKline (GSK), Ernst & Young, and Siemens are not just offering comprehensive programs for women; they are shifting their cultures to meet the needs of the new generation of workers where strong women are an essential force worldwide. To help you engage your top-talent women, I've listed ideas gleaned from these companies for you in the form of requests. Because I am speaking for most high-achieving women, I write from the voice of "we" so you can hear the larger call to action. Some of these ideas you can carry out as CEO. Some you can pass on to your managers. At the end of the list, I have a suggestion for how you can start the process of organizational transformation. I am at your service to help in this effort.

FROM OUR POINT OF VIEW: HOW TO ENGAGE AND RETAIN HIGH-ACHIEVING WOMEN

1. Provide Developmental Opportunities

One of our greatest passions is to resolve complex challenges, yet we need our managers to provide the resources for learning so we can be continually successful. We are top talent because we are committed to being the best. We come to you with experiences and degrees. To continue on our path to excellence, we need you to support the continuation of our development by offering ample tuition reimbursement and encouragement to further our learning. We want you to treat training and coaching programs not as perks but as a part of your overall business strategy. Frankly, to stay innovative and progressive, all employees should be trained in communication skills, managing change, dealing with their emotions, and building strong relationships with their peers within and across divisional borders. This is especially true in tough economic times when you need everyone to stay on top of their game. The last thing you want to do is cut funding for training and coaching when we are facing major difficulties. Give us more opportunities to learn and grow so we can help you take the company to the top faster than our competition. We would love for you to engage us in that challenge.

Also, provide us with mentors who are passionate about what they do so we are inspired to stay and learn more. We like to feel that we are in the company of smart and spirited people. We like to connect with leaders in other areas. We want breadth as well as depth of knowledge. If possible, create a platform where the most successful women in the company can network with and develop the younger female talent so the pipeline grows. Also, we are not always politically astute, so a good mentor can help us put our energies in the right places and see opportunities that we might miss that best use our talents.

2. *Make Our Mission Meaningful*

We want to be a part of something that feels bigger than ourselves. Even if our products are not that meaningful in the bigger scheme of life, we want to work for companies that care for their employees, respect the environment, and support their local communities. We will eventually disengage if we don't see how our work fits into a broader, more significant context. We struggle with committing to a monetary goal or a drive solely focused on beating our competitors. We don't just work to make a living. We work to make life better. We will align our energies with your penchant for profit when we can see the evidence of our good work in the world, even if that means we are simply helping people to feel more safe and happy. We know in our hearts we can make a significant difference on this planet. If we are doing that in our jobs, we are likely to stick around and share with the world how excited we are about our work.

3. Continually Affirm Our Contribution and Value

Our sense of contribution and value to the organization is as important to us as our paycheck, but we can't always see the larger effect of our work. We need to know how well we did in relation to the people we touch, whether it's our peers or our customers. It's not enough for us to know we have great knowledge and ability. We need to know if we have made an impact and that others value our involvement.

This acknowledgment needs to be continual because our sense of contribution is fleeting. Once we finish a task, we are quickly on to the next. There's always another project to master and another crisis for us to resolve. You need to remind us of our impact because we tend to lose this sense while swimming in the sea of our assignments.

However, don't overload us because you can count on us for results. We love to give outstanding performances. We love that you trust us. Yet if you rely on us too much, we would rather look for another job than face failure. Make sure to regularly ask us how we are feeling about our work and if we need any resources to get our work done. We often struggle with asking for help. Even when we ask to figure out a problem on our own, we still appreciate that you check in to see if we need any additional support.

4. Design and Foster a Creative and Collaborative Environment

We love to work for leaders who create environments that provide an open flow of communication in all directions. Let us talk freely, whether it's around the real water cooler or the virtual water cooler using social media. Environments that support collaboration foster rapid innovations. We want easy access to tools and resources. We want our leaders to be visionaries and catalysts who transfer decision-making to us and allow us to choose how we want to work. Instead of managing people from a top-down position, leaders should see themselves as the "spokesperson" in the middle of the wheel with employees in motion around them. They should inspire more than enforce. Cooperative cultures represent the future of management. We want to help you make this significant change.

5. Delegate Clear Expectations and Then Let Go

If you give us what we need to do a great job on work that is meaningful to us and valuable to the organization, we won't disappoint you. Give us control over the processes and decisions related to our tasks as much as possible. We love figuring out the best solutions. We need to feel we have the power to implement what we plan. If you think we need a more strategic perspective, coach us to see other possibilities instead of telling us what to do. When you delegate a project to us, give us the authority to talk to all stakeholders to negotiate actions. We will report our progress to you on a schedule we agree to and respond to issues promptly. We learn fast from our mistakes.

Let us know early on when changes will affect our work and share with us the reasons for the change. These days, those kinds of changes happen daily. We need to know about a shift in direction as soon as you do. If something comes up and you have to make a decision that goes counter to what we had hoped for, tell us why you made the decision so we can develop our business acumen. We want to grow beyond our technical capability. Letting us see through your eyes gives us what we need to succeed in our future positions.

6. Recognize Outstanding Performance

We like working for companies that have a culture of recognition. You may think that we are just doing our jobs, but we need to be recognized for our hard work even when it becomes the norm. Your recognition can be as simple as a personal comment or written note praising something we specifically did and the impact it had. We also like public recognition. When you visibly recognize our continual peak performance you demonstrate to everyone that you value this behavior. And don't just recognize results; show appreciation for our creativity, inclusiveness, optimism, and determination even if the results did not turn out as expected. When you honor our efforts, you help us to feel proud. We need help when it comes to stopping and admiring our work. If you give us this gift, we will repeat the behavior you reward.

Also, please recognize us by knowing us. We are staunchly loyal to the people who show they care about us now and in the future. Know our talents, goals, and dreams. If you were called by HR today and asked what you thought were my strengths, frustrations, and aspirations, could you answer these questions? Know who we are today and what we want for tomorrow. If we aren't clear about what we want for our careers, help us envision our future. Then offer to support us as we move forward on this path.

7. *Give Us Flexible Work Schedules*

We need help in managing our energy more than our time. We will work obsessively to complete important projects. Yet we need to renew our energy so we don't burn out. Therefore, we want flexible schedules based on meeting goals instead of wasting time in traffic or on "who can stay the latest" contests. We recognize the need to be present for important meetings, but on days we can get more work done from home, trust us. We have become comfortable with technology and will use it to communicate. Because we always produce results, let us figure out how we will get the work done. If you want to know more about setting up work cultures that are flexible and successful as a result, look at what these companies are doing: Capitol One, Deloitte & Touche, Best Buy, Marriott, Patagonia, AES Corporation, Sun Microsystems, IBM, PepsiCo, and Wal-Mart. At the Brazilian company Semco, employees choose their own salaries, set their own hours, and have no job titles, yet the profits keep growing and there is practically no employee turnover. By the time you read this, more companies will have followed suit. We're hoping you want to stay ahead of the pack with these progressive companies.

If we have children to take care of, don't put us on a "mommy track" that doesn't have access to promotions and plum assignments. Let us decide what we can handle. If you allow us the flexibility to meet the goals on our own terms, we will in turn be honest with you about what is possible. If we decide we need to step back because our home-life challenges need our attention, welcome us back when we are ready and we will amaze you with the results we produce.

When you stand back and look at the company you oversee, we hope you recognize how our requests serve your entire workforce. They could have been made by any employee who wants to feel more inspired at work and seeks more independence, inclusion, recognition, opportunities to learn, and control over his or her time. If you don't heed their needs, you will stifle their passion, curiosity, and creativity. We, the high-achieving women of your organization, won't stay where we feel held back, distrusted, and unappreciated. Most of the employees who will stay with you will do their jobs, but not much more.

It's time to let go of past ways of doing business to embrace new, more engaging structures. The design of the corporation came out of the Industrial Age, where it was most important to manage processes instead of people. Organizations needed to be lean, mean machines with zero defects. Recognition was based on numbers. Promotions were based on technical skill. Now, instead of managing processes, in the Technological Age, the Age of the Internet, the focus must shift to leading interconnected communities of people. Command-and-control power doesn't work in this environment. You can't command smart people to work harder. You can't make people collaborate. If you don't change the organizational structure and leadership styles to encourage internal networking and personal control over time and procedures, you will suffocate productivity. Sticking to the past will not bode well for the future in a competitive, global marketplace.

We propose an end to rigid hierarchy, to old paradigms, and to archaic terminology around measuring individual performances. Are you up to this challenge? Are you willing to do what it takes to engage employees today, to inspire and steer their energies to innovate and create extraordinary results together? This is your challenge today, to create the environment to engage both the hearts and minds of the new workforce. We all want developmental opportunities, meaningful work, a sense of personal contribution, collaborative work environments, more control over our work, recognition for our efforts, and flexible work schedules. The top women of your organization will stand by your side to help you make these changes. In fact, that may be your best use for us—empower teams of high-achieving women to create a new management structure and to solve the company's most pressing problems. We will attack these projects with gusto.

WHAT YOU CAN DO NOW

Coming from my personal perspective, I believe you should start by measuring existing engagement in the organization. If you don't have access to an assessment already, there are many tools available to measure the perceptions, attitudes, and opinions of employees. You can create your own simple online survey asking twenty questions. Below is a sample list of things you can put in a survey. Because most managers rank their top employees, I suggest you break out the results from your high achievers to determine how committed and happy your most talented employees are today. Then, as you implement changes in the organization, use the survey to monitor the results over time. Research has demonstrated that any change will get good results up front. You want to make sure the results are sustained. If they are not, I suggest you look deeper at the specific items that keep dropping below what is acceptable.

Here are some suggestions of items you can have employees rate to determine the level of their engagement in the organization. On a scale of 1 to 5, how would they rate:

- Their satisfaction with the organization as a place to work
- How often they consider working elsewhere
- How well the organization recognizes outstanding performance
- How much trust they feel from their managers
- How often they feel empowered
- How safe they feel to take risks and make mistakes
- How meaningful they feel their work is
- The level and frequency of challenges they are given to solve
- How often their manager includes them in decision-making
- How satisfied they are with their professional development
- How well they see a direct link in their job to the success of the organization
- How often management communicates with them directly and candidly
- To what level their boss feels as passionate about their work as they do
- How much input they have in setting their own goals
- How much input they have in setting their own schedules
- How much they feel cared about as a person
- The frequency and quality of feedback they receive

- How often they are recognized for effort as well as results
- If they have the right resources to do their work, and
- How well they trust that this survey will lead to positive changes in the organization

Once you tabulate the results, hold forums for discussions and idea-generation, preferably offsite, with different levels of people sitting at each table. You may need to do this over time to allow involvement by everyone or at least a strong representation of your entire workforce. The room should be free of distractions and be comfortable so people want to participate. Provide a summary of the survey results for everyone to read. Share case studies of what other companies are doing to increase engagement. Share the requests I made earlier in this letter. Then prompt the groups to have open dialogues about what they think the survey results mean and what changes could improve the results in the future. Give plenty of time to have frank discussions about what is possible in our organization. Encourage brainstorming. Discourage brain-stopping remarks about what can't happen here. Gather all ideas on paper.

With your employees' ideas in hand, use your executive team to identify action steps that can be taken now, what you can do within the upcoming year, and what will follow after that. You may focus on a few items at a time or develop a comprehensive plan depending on available resources. Be realistic about what is possible in order to manage everyone's expectations. Also, be clear on how the plan aligns with the business objectives so no one loses sight of the most important revenue goals. Finally, explain how the survey will be used in the future to monitor the success of the plan.

I know what I am asking for will not be easy, and you might think that now is not the time for making changes in leadership. The truth is that now is not the time to protect resources and tighten belts. Now is the time to make critical decisions to build talent within the organization and to court tomorrow's winners to join. It is time to play the offense on talent to ramp up your competitive advantage. This includes moving more women into your executive ranks. If you want to tap into the passion of your high-achieving women, retain them at full speed in your organization, and inspire them to take on executive positions, you have to take the necessary steps to better engage them now. It is time to meet their needs and provide them with good mentors and coaches to aid in their development.

The strategies outlined in this letter mean good business. "It is in everyone's best interest to bring qualified women into leadership positions, especially now when fresh perspectives are needed," said Ilene H. Lang, president and CEO of Catalyst. "What is good for women is good for men, business, and the global economy."[9] When you help more women climb the corporate ladder, the results will be good not only for your organization but for the world economy as well.

Sincerely,
(your name)

• • • •

TEN

A Tribe, or a Growing Revolution?

After I completed a speech for a large audience of women, a line quickly formed, blocking my exit from the stage. A slim, stylish woman in her fifties grabbed me by the wrist and declared, "I'm a Wander Woman." She proceeded to tell me about her adventures in what she called "job tasting" as she had tried out many professions in her career. She never suffered long in a job that didn't provide enough challenge and advancement. She now successfully sells marketing services to corporations. She thanked me for affirming the sanity of her zigzagging path. The next woman appeared to be in her early thirties. She invited me to a happy hour with her "all woman–all geek" networking group. The third woman whispered, "Is it okay to tell people at work that you like to wander?" I asked her if she had made herself invaluable to her team. "Oh, yes," she said, "that's why I think they would be terrified if they knew." I smiled and told her to keep asking for what makes her happy. They just might meet her demands. I spent the next half hour listening to women tell me how they clinched huge deals, launched new products, and broke through barriers while planning their next moves. They loved that I legitimized their journey and taught them how to turn their restlessness into a strategy.

There is no doubt in my mind that a powerful shift is taking place. Whether I am delivering a class in Chile, a seminar in Chicago, or a webinar with participants in Copenhagen, there's always a Wander Woman or two who seek my advice after class. Sometimes they just want to thank me for letting them know they are not alone. Their existence is evidence that the Wander Woman phenomenon is not an outgrowth of any particular culture.

Around the world, women are embracing their strength and hopping around jobs looking for the best place to shine. More women in their thirties and forties are pursuing operational, professional, and business management jobs instead of ancillary functions such as human resources to ensure they have an array of opportunities to choose from in the future. More women in their fifties are leveraging their experience by starting their own businesses. These women are redefining their relationships at home as well to better support the expression of their strengths and passion. No matter what they choose, they expect to be successful. They don't have to be like men. They expect men to accept them as the women they are. They are self-motivated, driven women who seek to have a significant impact on others, who are not afraid to try new things, who have a keen sense of relationship building, and who love instead of resist new challenges. There is a powerful shift taking place in the psyche of high-achieving women around the world.

Although many people have defined the persona of Wander Woman as a particular personality style, I believe the behavior of these women represents an emerging identity of women in general. Just as the development of women is a crucial factor in the advancement of a country, the counter effect is also true: as a society develops, so does the power of its women. For example, educating women leads to better childcare and health for the entire family.[1] This in turn means a stronger workforce and increased wealth for both men and women. As women gain economic parity with men, their confidence, independence, resilience, grit, and courage expand. They can define and go after their dreams, over and over again. Wander Women may represent a tribe that leads the way or they might be early adapters of women embracing a new identity. As women take their rightful place in the balance of world power, they may settle into their new sense of self and clout, quelling the restlessness that stirred them to rise up in the first place. Strong, passionate women may not wander once the structure of society and the design of organizational systems meet their needs.

Whether these women belong to a tribe or represent an emerging identity, it's critical that the leaders in our organizations meet the needs of today's high-achieving woman if they want to be the top revenue producers in their industries. These days, stock market successes belong to companies with women on their executive teams and boards of directors.[2] Yet the current generation of strong, smart, ambitious women will not fit into the fold of traditional corporate culture. They will stand up for themselves when demands are unreasonable. They will say no to standards and practices that do not serve their goals or the needs of their teams. The sooner leaders understand these women, honor their needs, and provide them with enough information to help them maneuver within their organizations, the sooner everyone benefits from the accomplishments these women will willingly provide. High-achieving women are vital organizational assets when it comes to moving strongly into the future. When organizational leaders understand this, the economy and our society as a whole will be stronger for it.

Unfortunately, most companies still operate with an old-fashioned view of women at work. As I write this in 2009, an article in the *New York Times* claims that women are hard-wired to bully each other, another article in the *Harvard Business Review* says women do not have the ability to spot big issues and inspire others to take action, and the federal courts are backlogged with work discrimination lawsuits, including ones where managers made decisions based on stereotypical beliefs that a woman's life situation naturally interferes with her ability to perform. I just received a ballot asking me to vote on which business speakers I would like to hear at an upcoming coaching conference. There wasn't one woman on the list.

This mindset won't change unless you—a strong, passionate, high-achieving woman—speak up until your viewpoints are acknowledged. It is time for you to leverage your value to your leaders by requesting them to take a new look at the women they employ. You have to put some of your powerful energy into changing people's minds about who today's high-achieving women really are. Leaders must recognize that there are many women who can make big-picture decisions, who want challenging job assignments, and who will happily support other women to grow at work. Although you may not be able to engage senior leaders face-to-face, you can chime in with the collective voice of today's high-achieving women by writing articles and blog posts, sending letters, and making your needs known at work.

In order to keep fueling the shifts in your workplace, you need to keep deepening your own self-understanding and resolve. Continually ask yourself what you want for your life. Find other women to dialogue with. Be aware of your behavior in making choices that align with your purpose. Free yourself from having to be great every moment so you can accept your whole self and allow the free flow of ideas to surface around you. Then, please, let yourself enjoy what is wonderful in your life right now. In the moments that you feel content, strong, and whole you can best take a stand for making the mindset changes in your companies and communities. The changes you help to make will better serve the human needs of all men and women.

You are leading the revolution. It needs your energy. Millions of women face the same dilemmas that you do every day. You have the right to say no to business as usual. When all strong, valuable women make their voices heard, we can tip the scales of power forever.

WANDER WOMEN UNITE

The day I was released from jail was bittersweet. Of course, I was ecstatic to get out. I was only twenty years old, yet the six months I had spent inside felt like a lifetime. I was a different person. I had learned many life lessons. Yet my cellmates, especially Vickie, had become a family I now had to leave behind. When I asked Vickie for a way to contact her in the future, she answered, "I don't want to see you again." I was shocked. When I reached out to touch her, she pulled away and said, "None of us want to see you, not where we're going. You have to move on. You have a story to tell. Out of all of us, you have the power to make a difference." I started to talk but she put her hand over my mouth. "Not here," she said. "Out there. Go change the world. Start a revolution if you want. That's what we want you to do. The next time we see your name, it will be in print."

At that moment I knew what it felt like to have someone believe in my powers so fully that she would cast me out into the world knowing I would thrive. Vickie didn't admire me for what grand things I had accomplished. She loved my courage, quick wit, determination, creativity, compassion, spunk, and passion. I know she had these traits, too. From the moment I met her, I was in awe of her strength. She taught me how women can honor each other for who we are, not what we do. When we can come to love this in each other and in ourselves, there's no stopping what we can do out in the world.

I believe in you, my high-achieving sister. I believe we can create communities of support where we help one another define our purpose, ask for what we need, test out new behaviors, be there when we stumble, and celebrate together when we win. Even if you don't want to change the larger world, we can work together to change your personal world to be more fulfilling. Whatever we do together serves all women, whether we are a tribe or societal trendsetters.

We are heroines on a journey that is easier walked together than alone. It's our time to have our voices heard. We can transform the world we live in. In the coming years, I hope to see your name listed as a business executive, famous entrepreneur, political power, or thought leader. I look forward to seeing your name in print.

NOTES ON THE RESEARCH

Although I have included stories and examples from women all over the world in this book, the women who participated in the interviews and surveys were part of a select group conforming to the research design for my doctoral dissertation. The scope was limited to women holding executive and managerial positions in U.S. corporations to maintain consistency of variables. Ten women were randomly chosen to be interviewed from a pool of seventy-five who matched the profile described below. Since the study, I have found many female managers, executives, entrepreneurs, and political leaders worldwide who also match the profile.

The women in the study were between the ages of twenty-eight and fifty-two with at least ten years of corporate experience. Drawing from a variety of sources, I concluded that women born in the twentieth century before 1955 were the trailblazers in the history of American corporations, marking the first generation of women to launch professional careers and fill management seats in numbers. Owing to the societal factors described in chapter 2, there was a dramatic shift in how girls were raised after 1955. When my research was completed in 2007, those born in 1955 were fifty-two years old.

The lower age limit of twenty-eight was chosen based on Daniel J. Levinson's classic life-stage analysis in his book *The Seasons of a Woman's Life*, which states that after the age of twenty-seven, women develop a more stable sense of self in response to their tasks and challenges.[1] Prior to that age, they are more impressionable from outside sources, their environment changes more frequently, and they experience more events that are new to them so they cannot rely on their own experiences for direction. Therefore, in addition to the limits of the study, most of the examples in this book were taken from women at least thirty years of age.

I then used my own clients, my newsletter subscriber list, and my broad network of executive coaches to locate women willing to participate in the study. Once a pool of women had been identified, they were given a short questionnaire to ascertain if they met the criteria for inclusion. They had to be the proper age and have at least ten years of corporate experience. If they matched, they were given a DISC Style Analysis Instrument assessment. To determine if they were a high achiever, they had to score at least 75 percent as a "D" (dominant, active, achievement-oriented) and less than 25 percent as an "S" (steady, passive, relationship-oriented).

I chose not to use academic degrees or salaries to qualify the participants. The study defines high achievement as a behavior, not as an accomplishment. Because the focus was to discover why women aren't selecting, being promoted into, or staying in executive positions, the results should apply to any high-achieving woman whether or not she has advanced degrees, officer titles, or makes an income of six figures or more.

This list of women who qualified for the study was demographically diverse. They were spread evenly between the ages of twenty-nine and fifty-two. A little more than half of the women were married. At least half of the married women were the breadwinners in their households. More than half of the married women had children. Most of the women had college degrees, with more than half of them holding or earning advanced degrees. Therefore, the research included mostly college-educated married and single women, both childless women and mothers with children, and women of color.

From the list, I randomly chose ten women to do in-depth interviews. All accepted. I interviewed them in person in six different cities.

Following the interviews, I created an online survey and sent it to the remaining sixty-five women to verify the themes found in the interviews. The response rate for the survey was 57 percent, which is a high response rate for an online survey. This process gave credibility to the responses. Since the initial research was completed, I have sent short surveys to the seventy-five participants plus twenty-five female coaches who fit the demographics, looking for clarifications or additional insights. Generally the response I get to these inquiries has been in the 70 percent range.

After completing the initial interviews and survey, I broke the patterns down to define both successful career practices and behaviors that might disrupt career development. The intent of the analysis was to discover and share the inner factors—the beliefs, needs, aspirations, traits, and choices—that are keeping this group of women from moving into executive positions.

What I discovered was that this group of women defined success very differently from the women who came before them. In fact, their issues didn't focus on how they could smash the glass ceiling and earn more executive positions. These women, by choice, moved all over the place, not just up. The themes I uncovered reflected the needs and desires they were hoping to have fulfilled by their work. If climbing the ladder in a company met their needs, they climbed. If not, they moved on.

When the research was completed, the title *Wander Woman* emerged to encompass the overall sense of what actions these women took and what emotions they felt as they looked around to get their needs met. This research provided the foundation material for this book. I have included many quotes from the original interviewees and survey participants. Their full names are not included to protect their identity. Yet I am eternally grateful for their permission to use their thoughts and revelations here in service to the millions of women this book can potentially help now and in years to come.

CHAPTER NOTES

PREFACE

1. Daniel Goleman, *Emotional Intelligence: Why It Can Matter More Than IQ* (New York: Bantam Books, 1995).
2. Margaret J. Wheatley, *Leadership and the New Science: Discovering Order in a Chaotic World*, 2nd ed. (San Francisco: Berrett-Koehler, 1999), pp. 173–175.

ONE

1. Pauline Rose Clance and Suzanne Imes, "The Imposter Phenomenon in High-Achieving Women: Dynamics and Therapeutic Intervention," *Psychotherapy Theory, Research and Practice* 15(3) (1978): 241.
2. Jean Hollands, *Same Game, Different Rules: How to Get Ahead Without Being a Bully Broad, Ice Queen, or Ms. Understood* (New York: McGraw-Hill, 2002), p. xii.
3. Douglas M. McCracken, "Winning the Talent War for Women," *Harvard Business Review* 78 (November/December 2000): 160–168.
4. Deloitte Research, *The Journey: Becoming the Standard of Excellence, Deloitte Touche Tohmatsu Worldwide Member Firms 2006 Review* (New York: DTT Global Communications, 2006), p. 26.
5. Connie Gersick and Kathy Kram, "High-Achieving Women at Midlife: An Exploratory Study," *Journal of Management Inquiry* 11(2) (June 2002): 104–127.
6. Sylvia Ann Hewlett and Carolyn Buck Luce, "Off-Ramps and On-Ramps: Keeping Talented Women on the Road to Success," *Harvard Business Review* 83(3) (2005): 43–51. The article differentiates the "zigzag" pattern in women's career

paths from the vertical ascent up the corporate ladder that most men take. The reasons women leave jobs are detailed on page 49.

7. Anna Fels, "Do Women Lack Ambition?" *Harvard Business Review* 82(4) (2004): 57. Fels argues for a new definition of ambition because women are more likely than men to move on when the goals aren't appealing regardless of the titles or money offered.
8. Gersick and Kram, "High-Achieving Women at Midlife." On pages 120–122 the differences in career choices and paths between men and women are explained, including the fact that (1) women still face more frustration in the workplace when it comes to getting equal pay, equal recognition, and equal chances for the best opportunities and challenges, so they leave instead of living with their frustrations; (2) many women have found creative ways to invest in both career and family as they choose to move around more than men, who tend to plan their careers along a more traditional path; and (3) as women get older and their desires to learn and to make a difference outside of the home increase—partly owing to their children growing up and partly because of the tangible gain in experience and wisdom—they are more inclined to move around than men to find career opportunities that meet their need for new challenges and contribution and to find companies that align with their values.
9. Center for Women's Business Research, *Women-Owned Businesses in 2004: Trends in the U.S. and 50 States* (McLean, Va.: Center for Women's Business Research, 2005), p. 1.
10. Quoted in Heidi Brown, *On Her Own Terms*, Forbes.com, April 1, 2009. Available at: http://www.forbes. com/2009/04/01/workplace-career-ladder-women-power-executive.html.

TWO

1. Ina Wagner and Ruth Wodak, "Performing Success: Identifying Strategies of Self-Presentation in Women's Biographical Narratives," *Discourse & Society* 17(3) (2006): 385–411. Pages 406–407 provide examples of ways women are rewriting their definitions of success.
2. Marian N. Ruderman and Patricia J. Ohlott, *Standing at the*

Crossroads: Next Steps for High-Achieving Women (San Francisco: Jossey-Bass, 2002), pp. 120–121.

3. Jean M. Twenge, *Generation Me: Why Today's Young Americans Are More Confident, Assertive, Entitled—And More Miserable Than Ever Before* (New York: Free Press, 2006). Pages 55–56 explore how self-importance became mandatory for both parents and schools.
4. Liz Funk, *Supergirls Speak Out: Inside the Secret Crisis of Overachieving Girls* (New York: Touchstone, 2009).
5. S.L. Bem, *The Lenses of Gender: Transforming the Debate on Sexual Inequality* (New Haven, Conn.: Yale University Press, 1993).
6. Olfat Haddad, "Goal! A Woman Sportscaster in Gaza," *Menassat*, October 9, 2008.
7. National Center for Education Statistics, *Digest of Education Statistics* (2007), table 177. The study was documented by Mary Ann Mason, "Better Educating Our New Breadwinners: Creating Opportunities for All Women to Succeed in the Workforce," in *The Shriver Report: A Woman's Nation Changes Everything*, edited by Heather Boushey and Ann O'Leary (Maria Shriver and the Center for American Progress, 2009), pp. 161–193.
8. Quoted in Ben Feller, "Women Gaining on Men in Advanced Fields," Associated Press, June 1, 2006.
9. European Commission Directorate-General for Research, *She Figures 2006: Women and Science Statistics and Indicators* (Luxembourg: Office for Official Publications of the European Communities, 2006), p. 17.
10. The National Committee Secretariat, *National Report on Women in the Islamic Republic of Iran* (Tehran: Bureau of Women's Affairs, Office of the President of the Republic, May 1995), available at http://www.telecom.net.et/~iranet/page31.htm.
11. Justin Pope, "Women's Colleges Grow Abroad, Decline in the U.S.," Associated Press, June 10, 2008.
12. Carl Jung, "On the Psychology of the Unconscious" (1917), in *Two Essays on Analytical Psychology*, 2nd ed., translated by R.F.C. Hull (Princeton, N.J.: Princeton University Press, 1966), p. 53.

13. Margaret Mitchell, *Gone With the Wind* (New York: MacMillan Company, 1936), chapter 9.

THREE

1. Kenneth J. Gergen, *The Saturated Self: Dilemmas of Identity in Contemporary Life* (New York: Basic Books, 1991), p. 7.
2. Joseph LeDoux, *The Synaptic Self: How Our Brains Become Who We Are* (New York: Penguin Putnam, 2002), pp. 323–324.
3. Caroline Myss, *Sacred Contracts: Awakening Your Divine Potential* (New York: Three Rivers Press, 2002), p. 364. See also Myss's companion work, *Archetype Cards and Guidebook* (Carlsbad, Calif.: Hay House, 2003).
4. Jim Curtan teaches workshops and provides personal coaching using archetypal narratives to empower yourself and embrace change. You can contact Jim at jimcurtan@cmed.com.
5. Myss, *Archetype Cards and Guidebook*, p. 6.
6. Michael Jones, "Transforming Leadership Through the Power of the Imagination," *Integral Leadership Review* 9(2) (March 2009); see www.IntegralLeadershipReview.com.
7. The Pyramid Resource Group has coaches who have been trained to work with archetypes when coaching women leaders and high achievers. You can learn more about this corporate coaching company at www.PyramidResource.com, or e-mail DJ@PyramidResource.com.

FOUR

1. Liz Kahn, *The LPGA: The Unauthorized Version* (South Bend, Ind.: Diamond Communications, 1994). p. 142.
2. Robert M. Sapolsky, *Why Zebras Don't Get Ulcers: An Updated Guide to Stress, Stress-Related Diseases and Coping* (New York: W. H. Freeman, 1998), pp. 12–13. Dr. Sapolsky suggests our normal workdays trigger our stress response on a continual instead of intermittent basis, causing the stress response itself to suppress some systems while overactivating others.
3. Ibid., pp. 283–286. Sapolsky provides evidence that people who seem to control their emotions well are often just suppressing the expression of emotion, not the physiological re-

action in the body. In fact, the act of suppressing emotions takes a lot of energy, which detracts from cognitive functions such as memory, empathy, and positive emotions, as well as compromising the immune and cardiovascular systems.

4. John J. Ratey, *The User's Guide to the Brain* (New York: Pantheon Books, 2001). On pages 296–299, Ratey discusses what happens when the social functions of the brain are either not developed or suppressed. He then explores the brain's capacity to regenerate neural connections to better feel empathy and joy in social situations.
5. Frank McAndrew, "The Science of Gossip: Why We Can't Stop Ourselves," *Scientific American Mind* 19(6) (October 2008): 26–33.
6. Kathy Caprino, *Breakdown, Breakthrough: The Professional Woman's Guide to Claiming a Life of Passion, Power, and Purpose* (San Francisco: Berrett-Koehler, 2008), pp. 180–181. Caprino identifies the "overfunctioner" role in a woman who cleans up for the cleaning lady and who "saves time" by doing tasks that she assumes she would have to redo anyway if she gave the task away.
7. Robert W. Fuller, *Somebodies and Nobodies: Overcoming the Abuse of Rank* (Gabriela Island, B.C.: New Society Publishers, 2003), p. 2.
8. See Ann MacDonald, "Mental Concerts: What Neural 'Notes' Reveal About Consciousness and Creativity," The Dana Foundation's *Brain Work*, November 1, 2005, http://www.dana.org/news/brainwork/detail.aspx?id=766.
9. Daniel Goleman, *Social Intelligence: The New Science of Human Relationships* (New York: Bantam Books, 2006), pp. 268–269. Goleman describes how good moods heighten our cognitive functioning, creating "an optimal state" of mind.
10. Marion Woodman, *Addiction to Perfection: The Still Unravished Bride* (Toronto: Inner City Books, 1982).

FIVE

1. Joseph LeDoux, *The Emotional Brain* (New York: Touchstone, 1998), pp. 269–270.
2. John Medina, *Brain Rules* (Seattle: Pear Press, 2008), p. 235.

3. Louann Brizendine, *The Female Brain* (New York: Morgan Roads Books, 2006), p. 36.
4. Candace B. Pert, *Molecules of Emotion* (New York: Touchstone, 1999), p. 305.
5. William Bridges, *Transitions: Making Sense of Life's Changes* (Cambridge, Mass.: Da Capo Press, 2004), pp. 14–15, 125.
6. Appreciative Inquiry Commons, http://appreciativeinquiry.case.edu, is an Internet portal hosted by Case Western Reserve University's Weatherhead School of Management. The site is devoted to sharing definitions, research, case studies, visions, academic resources, and practical tools on Appreciative Inquiry.
7. Tristine Rainer, *The New Diary: How to Use a Journal for Self-Guidance and Expanded Creativity* (New York: Tarcher, 2004), pp. 3–5.
8. Many resources exist explaining how Appreciative Inquiry works and describing its uses. I found one of the most useful books to be Sue Annis Hammond's, *The Thin Book of Appreciative Inquiry*, 2nd ed. (Bend, Ore.: Thin Book Publishing, 1998). You can find the book at www.thinbook.com.
9. Ibid., p. 30.
10. John W. Gardner, *Self-Renewal: The Individual and the Innovative Society* (New York: Harper Colophon, 1965), p. 13.
11. Marcia Reynolds, *Outsmart Your Brain! How to Make Success Feel Easy* (Phoenix, Ariz.: Covisioning, 2004). The Relax-Detach-Center-Focus technique is described on pages 52–60. You can find the book at www.outsmartyourbrain.com.
12. Gary Austin teaches improvisation workshops. You can find his contact information at www.garyaustin.net/contact.html.
13. Dr. Tom Kubistant is a sports psychologist currently specializing in the mental game of golf. He can be found at http://www.psychologyofgolf.com.

SIX

1. Cathleen Falsani, "Interview with Illinois State Senator Barack Obama," March 27, 2004. At the time, Falsani was a religious reporter for the *Chicago Sun Times*. The inter-

view can be seen in its entirety at http://blog.beliefnet.com/stevenwaldman/2008/11/obamas-interview-with-cathleen.html.

2. Laura Berman Fortgang, *The Little Book on Meaning: Why We Crave It, How We Create It* (New York: Tarcher/Penguin, 2009), pp. 10–11. Fortgang, a renowned pioneer in the field of life coaching, chronicles her own journey and struggles to find meaning and provides profound insights from the instruction she received becoming an ordained interfaith minister.
3. Ibid., p. 48.
4. Carl G. Jung, *Modern Man in Search of a Soul*, translated by W. S. Dell and Cary F. Baynes (New York: Harcourt Harvest, 1955), pp. 108–111.
5. Daniel Gilbert, *Stumbling on Happiness* (New York: Vintage Books, 2007), pp. 83–105.
6. Ibid., pp. 137–138.
7. Dr. Clarissa Pinkola Estés, *Women Who Run with the Wolves* (New York: Random House, 1992), pp. 256–297.

SEVEN

1. William Bridges, *Transitions: Making Sense of Life's Changes* (Cambridge, Mass.: Da Capo Press, 2004), p. 4.
2. Ibid., pp. 133–155. Bridges provides the best description I have found for the gray phase of transformation between endings and beginnings in this chapter, titled "The Neutral Zone."
3. Victor Turner, "Betwixt and Between: The Liminal Period in *Rites de Passage*," in *The Forest of Symbols: Aspects of Ndembu Ritual* (Ithaca, N.Y.: Cornell University Press, 1967), pp. 96–97.
4. Ibid., p. 97.
5. Joseph Campbell, *Myths to Live By* (New York: Bantam, 1973), pp. 208–209.
6. Jonathan B. Spira and David M. Goldes, *Information Overload: We Have Met the Enemy and He Is Us* (New York: Basex, February 2007), pp. 3, 10.
7. "Jennifer Lerner on Emotion, Judgment and Public Policy,"

an interview with Jennifer Lerner conducted by Doug Gavel on February 14, 2008, and posted on the Harvard Kennedy School Web site, http://www.hks.harvard.edu/news-events/publications/insight/management/jennifer-lerner.

8. Robert M. Sapolsky, *Why Zebras Don't Get Ulcers: An Updated Guide to Stress, Stress-Related Diseases and Coping* (New York: W. H. Freeman, 1998), p. 308.
9. Doc Childre and Howard Martin, *The HeartMath Solution* (San Francisco: HarperSanFrancisco, 2000), pp. 33–34.
10. Timothy D. Wilson, *Strangers to Ourselves: Discovering the Adaptive Unconscious* (Cambridge, Mass.: Harvard University Press, 2002), pp. 93–115, 174–175.
11. Peggy Klaus, "A Sisterhood of Workplace Infighting," *New York Times*, January 11, 2009.
12. Shelley E. Taylor, Laura C. Klein, Brian P. Lewis, Tara L. Gruenewald, Regan A. Gurung, and John A. Updegraff, "Biobehavioral Responses to Stress in Females: Tend-and-Befriend, Not Fight-or-Flight," *Psychological Review* 107(3) (July 2000): 411–429.
13. Quoted in Ellen Michaud, "Women, Stress and Friendship," *Prevention Magazine*. Reprinted with permission at http://www.learningplaceonline.com/change/women/stress-friendship.htm.
14. Malcolm Gladwell, *Outliers: The Story of Success* (New York: Little, Brown, 2008), p. 115.
15. Robert Sapolsky, "Open Season," *The New Yorker*, March 30, 1998, p. 57. Dr. Sapolsky is a MacArthur "Genius" Fellow and a professor of biology and neurology at Stanford University. This article is a delightful summation of small studies he performed to explore why we reject novelty as we age.
16. Alfred Adler, *Social Interest: A Challenge to Mankind* (Oxford: Oneworld Publications, 1998), pp. 2–3.
17. Ibid., p. 3.

EIGHT

1. Dan McCarthy, *Would Your Peers Vote for You?* Great Leadership Blog, May 26, 2009, http://www.greatleadershipbydan.com/2009/05/would-your-peers-vote-for-you. html.

2. Scott Eblin, *The Next Level: What Insiders Know About Executive Success* (Boston: Davies-Black, 2006), p. 137.
3. Aristotle, *Nicomachean Ethics*, translated by David Ross (New York: Oxford University Press, 2009), book 2, 1109a25, p. 36.
4. Claire Shipman and Katty Kay, *Womenomics: Write Your Own Rules for Success* (New York: HarperCollins, 2009), p. 144.
5. Marcia Reynolds, "The Water We Swim In: A New Look at Cognitive Evolution," *The International Journal of Coaching in Organizations* 2 (2006): 46. Both the budget example and the differentiating factors between Achievers and Perceivers (tactical versus strategic thinking) are described in the article.
6. Gary Hamel, *The Future of Management* (Boston: Harvard Business School Press, 2007), pp. 229–239.
7. Shipman and Kay, *Womenomics*, p. xxii. Kay and Shipman introduce the concept of "The New All" for women.
8. Marcia Reynolds, *Capture the Rapture: How to Step Out of Your Head and Leap into Life* (Scottsdale, Ariz.: Hathor Hill Press, 2000), pp. 107–108.
9. Cheryl Richardson, *Life Makeovers: 52 Practical & Inspiring Ways to Improve Your Life One Week at a Time* (New York: Broadway Books, 2002). The process is explained on pp. 6–7. Cheryl also has a weekly Coach on Call program where you can get your questions answered, plus online e-learning programs at http://www.cherylrichardson.com.

NINE

1. Linda Tarr-Wheelan, *Women Lead the Way: Your Guide to Stepping Up to Leadership and Changing the World* (San Francisco: Berrett-Koehler, 2009). Tarr-Wheelan cites seven research reports and conference proceedings on pages 23–24 and lists the references on page 183.
2. Roy D. Adler, *Women in the Executive Suite Correlate to High Profits*, Pepperdine University, European Project on Equal Pay, p. 5. Retrieved from http://www.women2top.net/download/home/adler_web.pdf.
3. McKinsey and Company, *Women Matter: Gender Diversity,*

A Corporate Performance Driver (Paris: McKinsey and Company, 2007), pp. 12–14.

4. Ernst & Young, *Groundbreakers: Using the Strength of Women to Rebuild the Global Economy*, paper delivered at the World Economic Forum, Davos, Switzerland, 2009. The full text starting with the executive summary can be viewed at http://www.ey.com/GL/en/Issues/Driving-growth/Groundbreakers---Executive-Summary.
5. Ann Howard and Richard S. Wellins, *Holding Women Back*, a report from DDI's Global Leadership Forecast 2008/2009, pp. 7–8. The full text of the report can be found at http://www.ddiworld.com/pdf/GenderReport09_tr_ddi.pdf.
6. Chris Petersen, "Breaking Through: Why Are So Few Women in Leadership Roles?" *U.S. Business Review* 9(4) (April 2008): 7.
7. Sylvia Ann Hewlett and Carolyn Buck Luce, "Off-Ramps and On-Ramps: Keeping Talented Women on the Road to Success," *Harvard Business Review* 83(3) (January 2005): 43–51.
8. National Center for Education Statistics, *Digest of Education Statistics* (2007), table 177. The study was documented by Mary Ann Mason, "Better Educating Our New Breadwinners: Creating Opportunities for All Women to Succeed in the Workforce," in *The Shriver Report: A Woman's Nation Changes Everything*, edited by Heather Boushey and Ann O'Leary (Maria Shriver and the Center for American Progress, 2009), pp. 161–193.
9. Ernst & Young, *Groundbreakers: Using the Strength of Women to Rebuild the Global Economy.* The quote can be viewed at http://www.ey.com/GL/en/Issues/Driving-growth/Groundbreakers---The-power-of-critical-mass.

TEN

1. UNESCO, "Gender and Education for All: The Leap to Equality," *EFA Global Monitoring Report 2003/04*, executive summary, chapter 1. The text can be downloaded at http://portal.unesco.org/education/en/ev.php-URL_ID=24284&URL_DO=DO_TOPIC&URL_SECTION=201.html.
2. Lois Joy, "The Bottom Line: Corporate Performance and Women's Representation on Boards," *Catalyst*, October 2007.

The report can be downloaded at http://www.catalyst.org/publication/200/the-bottom-line-corporate-performance-and-womens-representation-on-boards.

NOTES ON THE RESEARCH

1. Daniel J. Levinson, *Seasons of a Woman's Life* (New York: Ballantine Books, 1996), pp. 97, 117.

ACKNOWLEDGMENTS

Recently, a gentleman sat with me at lunch at the International Coach Federation (ICF) conference. He asked me to share with him how I built my business. I told him, "I publicly state an intention and my community shows up to help." While I was researching and writing this book, many cheerleaders kept me on the path even when I questioned my choices. To this day, I am so grateful every time a colleague touts my book and a new acquaintance opens a door for me to speak. Thank you. I may not have named you here, but know that I am thankful beyond words for your support. How lucky I am to know you.

First, I have to thank Johanna Vondeling, my editor, for hearing the kernels of my ideas and believing in them, and me, so much that she walked me through the process of cultivating them into a book. Her belief in me has brought me to tears many times, even though her rigor often balanced my joy with a good dose of humility. I am lucky that I fortuitously sat next to her at the ICF conference in Montreal.

Johanna led me to the world of Berrett-Koehler, where I met the president, Steve Piersanti. I never imagined a publishing company could have such heart. I am honored to be a part of a concerned and caring family that calls itself a business.

Back to my coaching community, if it weren't for the late Thomas Leonard, founder of Coach U and the ICF, I might never have found the path to coaching. Sandy Vilas has kept Coach U going and growing, which has connected me to amazing coaches around the world. Thanks to Sandy and Thomas, I have a global community of friends that I know will last my lifetime.

I am forever amazed at the current and past presidents and board members of the International Coach Federation who continue to care and serve. You inspire my dedication to the coaching profession. I hope this book is a welcome resource to the coaching community.

D.J. Mitsch, president of the Pyramid Resource Group, has been a model of courage for me. She is a light bearer even in the most frenetic, fearful, and angry corporate worlds. I will follow her anywhere. I am also grateful for the Pyramid coaches who are just as much my brothers and sisters as my blood family.

Zoran Todorovic, president of TNM Coaching in Copenhagen, opened many possibilities for my work on a global level. Because of Zoran, I have led leadership classes in twelve countries on five continents, giving me a perspective and an education I could not have gotten from any school. He, too, has given me a family of coaches who are dedicated to transforming the world. I will wake up at any hour to meet and conspire with the TNM team. And Vivienne Ladommatou—I often wonder when our souls first met.

I have had my own coaches along the way who have all helped me stand in the space I am in today—Harriett Simon Salinger, Margaret Krigbaum, Joeann Fossland, Linley Rose, and Jeff Raim. Harriett, you always remind me who I am when I forget, keeping my fires burning.

Jim Curtan's clear articulation of the archetypes and his expert coaching helped me to create the concept of our "circle of selves" and write the exercises that make this body of work relevant and accessible to the readers.

Vickie Sullivan gave me the green light to focus my business on high-achieving women. She is a marketing strategist extraordinaire. When she told me my focus was brilliant, I knew I was on to something good.

It was a pleasure meeting the women who participated in my research, especially the ten who allowed me to show up in their towns and spend hours with me as I probed about their lives, joys, disappointments, and dreams. They gave me the foundation for this book and my future work. Together, we are making a difference.

Thanks to Agi Mura, who talked me into going to the Professional School of Psychology for my doctorate, and to Dr. William Bergquist, whose deep well of wisdom kept me inspired throughout the entire program and dissertation process.

Karl Schnell, my life partner, is my knight. He unconditionally supports me and my work even when I am called to travel thousands of miles away. He then cares for our home, allowing me to comfortably rest, rejuvenate, and obsess again between my journeys. When he can break away from his own business, he joins me on my travels, reminding me that living is about playing as well as working. His patience and big heart are the threads of our relationship.

My life pals, Debbie Basehore and Wendy White, reserve a special place in my heart. Wendy was the first Wander Woman in my life. Watching her express her adventurous spirit allowed me to honor mine. Debbie was our base. No matter where our lives took us, Debbie was always there when we needed her.

The other cheerleaders I must mention are Alice Adams-Sax, Toni Koch, Jennie Layne Keller, Linda Lunden, Megan McCoy, Diana Sterling, and, especially, my soul sister Sherry Kilian and soul brother Paul Jantzi.

Finally, I thank my family—my brothers, Harold and David, who never fail to make me laugh, and my sister, Eve, who keeps a sense of family alive. In them, I can still see my late parents—my mother who laughed until she cried and my father who challenged me to be not just the glitter, but the guiding light of a star. I would never have reached this place without the bond of love my parents provided. I am still hoping to make them both proud.

INDEX

ABOUT THE AUTHOR

Marcia Reynolds, Psy.D.

Master Certified Coach

Author photo: Tina Celle

Dr. Marcia Reynolds is fascinated by the brain, especially what triggers enthusiasm and innovation in the workplace. This fascination has led her down many roads in her desire to stay on top of the shifts in employee engagement and leadership development. On this journey, she has developed and woven together three areas of expertise: organizational change, coaching, and emotional intelligence. She is able to draw on these areas as she works with her latest passion—helping high-achieving women examine and strategize their full and amazing lives.

Her first expertise, organizational change, developed out of necessity when facing the challenges of running corporate training departments in the 1980s and 1990s. Her greatest success story came as a result of designing the employee development program for a semiconductor manufacturing company facing bankruptcy. As she worked with the executive staff, the company not only turned around, but also became the top IPO in the country in 1993. During this time she learned the power of teamwork over individual contribution and the importance of having a compelling vision for yourself and for your organization. These insights, along with suggestions and exercises, are included in the book.

As a corporate trainer, Marcia experienced the typical frustration of watching people participate with gusto in training classes and then, when back on the job, apply very little of what they learned. In her search for new techniques, she enrolled in a coaching school in 1995 when she started her own business. She quickly saw the power of coaching to make the mental shifts required before behavioral change can occur. Her passion for the profession led her to hold the position of president of the International Coach Federation in 2000 and become one of the first twenty people in the world to hold the certification of Master Certified Coach. She now coaches executives and teaches coaching in her leadership classes worldwide. She has woven in powerful coaching questions throughout this book to both motivate and maintain the reader's commitment to change.

At the same time that Marcia found coaching, she discovered and became absorbed in learning about emotional intelligence (EI). She then designed and taught courses around the world. She was the first to teach EI in Russia, Kenya, and for the agencies in the U.S. National Institutes of Health. Her curiosity led her to dig deeper into the brain research that was redefining how we learn and evolve. To satisfy her hunger for knowing more, she chose to get her doctorate in organizational psychology, complementing her two master's degrees in communications and adult learning. Every paper she wrote gave her deeper insights into her own life choices as well as to the struggles many of her female coaching clients were experiencing. Her doctoral work helped her to define "the burden of greatness" that high achievers now experience and the steps for Appreciative Dialogue to help them resolve their urgent issues. These are crucial concepts in this book. Throughout the pages she shares illuminating stories, quotes, and themes from her dissertation research on high-achieving women.

Excerpts from Marcia's book *Outsmart Your Brain* have appeared in many places, including *Harvard Management Review*, *Cosmopolitan*, and the *New York Times*, and she has appeared on *ABC World News*. She has written numerous articles for the *International Journal of Coaching in Organizations*. Marcia is also a dynamic keynote speaker and has earned the designation of Certified Speaking Professional. You can read more about Marcia on her Web sites, http://www.WanderWomanBook.com and http://www.outsmartyourbrain.com. Marcia travels the world from her hometown of Phoenix, Arizona.

ABOUT BERRETT-KOEHLER PUBLISHERS

Berrett-Koehler is an independent publisher dedicated to an ambitious mission: Creating a World That Works for All.

We believe that to truly create a better world, action is needed at all levels—individual, organizational, and societal. At the individual level, our publications help people align their lives with their values and with their aspirations for a better world. At the organizational level, our publications promote progressive leadership and management practices, socially responsible approaches to business, and humane and effective organizations. At the societal level, our publications advance social and economic justice, shared prosperity, sustainability, and new solutions to national and global issues.

A major theme of our publications is "Opening Up New Space." They challenge conventional thinking, introduce new ideas, and foster positive change. Their common quest is changing the underlying beliefs, mindsets, and structures that keep generating the same cycles of problems, no matter who our leaders are or what improvement programs we adopt.

We strive to practice what we preach—to operate our publishing company in line with the ideas in our books. At the core of our approach is stewardship, which we define as a deep sense of responsibility to administer the company for the benefit of all of our "stakeholder" groups: authors, customers, employees, investors, service providers, and the communities and environment around us.

We are grateful to the thousands of readers, authors, and other friends of the company who consider themselves to be part of the "BK Community." We hope that you, too, will join us in our mission.

A BK LIFE BOOK

This book is part of our BK Life series. BK Life books change people's lives. They help individuals improve their lives in ways that are beneficial for the families, organizations, communities, nations, and world in which they live and work. To find out more, visit www.bk-life.com.

Be Connected

VISIT OUR WEBSITE

Go to www.bkconnection.com to read exclusive previews and excerpts of new books, find detailed information on all Berrett-Koehler titles and authors, browse subject-area libraries of books, and get special discounts.

SUBSCRIBE TO OUR FREE E-NEWSLETTER

Be the first to hear about new publications, special discount offers, exclusive articles, news about bestsellers, and more! Get on the list for our free e-newsletter by going to www.bkconnection.com.

GET QUANTITY DISCOUNTS

Berrett-Koehler books are available at quantity discounts for orders of ten or more copies. Please call us toll-free at (800) 929-2929 or email us at bkp.orders@aidcvt.com.

HOST A READING GROUP

For tips on how to form and carry on a book reading group in your workplace or community, see our website at www.bkconnection.com.

JOIN THE BK COMMUNITY

Thousands of readers of our books have become part of the "BK Community" by participating in events featuring our authors, reviewing draft manuscripts of forthcoming books, spreading the word about their favorite books, and supporting our publishing program in other ways. If you would like to join the BK Community, please contact us at bkcommunity@bkpub.com.

Produced by Wilsted & Taylor Publishing Services
Copyediting by Nancy Evans
Design and composition by Yvonne Tsang
Proofreading and indexing by Andrew Joron